BLESS ME,
ULTIMA

Rudolfo A. Anaya

SPARKNOTES is a registered trademark of SparkNotes LLC.

Spark Publishing
A Division of Barnes & Noble
120 Fifth Avenue
New York, NY 10011
www.sparknotes.com

ISBN-13: 978-1-5866-3500-8
ISBN-10: 1-5866-3500-X

Please submit changes or report errors to www.sparknotes.com/errors.

Printed and bound in the United States

7   9   10   8

Introduction:
Stopping to Buy SparkNotes on a Snowy Evening

Whose words these are you *think* you know.
Your paper's due tomorrow, though;
We're glad to see you stopping here
To get some help before you go.

Lost your course? You'll find it here.
Face tests and essays without fear.
Between the words, good grades at stake:
Get great results throughout the year.

Once school bells caused your heart to quake
As teachers circled each mistake.
Use SparkNotes and no longer weep,
Ace every single test you take.

Yes, books are lovely, dark, and deep,
But only what you grasp you keep,
With hours to go before you sleep,
With hours to go before you sleep.

CONTENTS

CONTEXT

Rudolfo Anaya was born on October 30, 1937, in Pastura, New Mexico, the fifth of seven children. Anaya also had three half-siblings from his parents' previous marriages. When Anaya was still very young, his family moved to Santa Rosa, New Mexico. When he was a teenager, his family moved again, this time to Albuquerque, where Anaya graduated from high school in 1956. He attended business school for two years and dropped out before finishing, but he graduated from the University of New Mexico a few years later. Anaya worked as a public school teacher in Albuquerque from 1963 to 1970. During that period, he married Patricia Lawless. Afterward, he worked as the director of counseling for the University of Albuquerque for two years before accepting a position as an associate professor at the University of New Mexico.

When Anaya was a freshman in college, he began writing poetry and novels. His wife encouraged him to pursue his literary endeavors, and over a period of seven years, he completed his first and best-known novel, *Bless Me, Ultima*. East Coast publishing houses rejected the novel repeatedly. Finally, in 1972, a group of Chicano publishers accepted his book. *Bless Me, Ultima* went on to win the prestigious Premio Quinto Sol award and is now considered a classic Chicano work.

Bless Me, Ultima is the story of a young boy's coming-of-age within a cultural tapestry that includes Spanish, Mexican, and Native American influences, and in which many of the major cultural forces conflict with one another. The young boy, Antonio Márez, must navigate a number of conflicts—between farmers and cowboys, Spanish and indigenous peoples, and English-speaking and Spanish-speaking peoples—that collectively structured the cultural life in rural New Mexico during the 1940s. The novel is also semiautobiographical. Like Antonio's parents, Anaya's mother was the daughter of farmers and his father was a vaquero, or cowboy. In his teens, Anaya suffered a serious swimming injury that left him temporarily paralyzed. This incident appears in *Bless Me, Ultima* when Florence, Antonio's friend, dies in a swimming accident. Like Antonio's family, Anaya's family respected the art of curanderismo, or folk medicine, which Ultima practices throughout the book. Anaya and his siblings moved between the Spanish-and English-speaking worlds, and they were raised in a devoutly Catholic home, like the Márez children were. And like Antonio's brothers, Anaya's brothers were fighting in World War II during most of his early childhood.

Anaya has become a prominent Chicano intellectual and writer since the publication of *Bless Me, Ultima*. He has given lectures at many colleges and has won several literary awards for his work. Over the years, he has demonstrated a strong commitment to helping new Chicano writers through the difficult and sometimes daunting process of getting their voices heard.

PLOT OVERVIEW

WHEN ANTONIO MÁREZ is almost seven years old, the old healer Ultima comes to stay with him and his family in their small house in Guadalupe, New Mexico. The family has taken in Ultima out of a respect for her healing powers, her knowledge of plant lore, and her long use of folk magic in service of the community. Though they have great respect for Ultima's spirituality, the family, especially Antonio's mother, is devoutly Catholic. Antonio's father, Gabriel, is a former vaquero, or cowboy, who wandered the llano, the great plains of New Mexico. Antonio's mother, María, is the daughter of farmers. Antonio's parents now argue about their young son's future; Gabriel hopes he will become a vaquero on the llano, and María hopes he will become a priest. When he was born, Ultima served as his midwife and buried his afterbirth. As a result, it is now thought that she alone knows what lies in Antonio's future.

Antonio spends a happy time with Ultima, learning about plants and trees and helping her gather herbs on the llano. One night, his innocence is threatened when he witnesses the death of Lupito, a soldier who recently returned from World War II. Lupito is shot to death by a mob after he kills the sheriff in a moment of post-traumatic delirium. After seeing Lupito's death, Antonio begins to wonder about sin, death, and hell. Antonio walks to church with Ultima the next morning, and she tells him that each person must make his or her own moral choices, must choose a set of values to use to understand the world.

That fall, after helping his mother's brothers, the Lunas, with their harvest, Antonio begins school. María presses Ultima to reveal Antonio's destiny, and she replies sadly that he will be a man of learning. The war ends, and Antonio's brothers return home. Gabriel is overjoyed because he hopes the return of his older sons means that the family will at last be able to move to California, as he has longed to do. But the brothers are surly, restless, and traumatized by the war. Before long, they each leave home to pursue independent lives. Antonio struggles to understand the conflict between his father and his brothers, but like so many of the moral questions that trouble him, it is too complicated for him to grasp. His mother tells him that he will

3

understand when he begins to take Communion, and he begins to look forward anxiously to the day he will be old enough to do so.

Antonio's friend Samuel takes him fishing and tells him the story of the golden carp, a river god who looks out for mankind. Antonio is moved by the story, but he does not know how to reconcile it with his Catholic beliefs. His beliefs are challenged again when his uncle Lucas is cursed by the satanic Trementina sisters. The priest is unable to cure him, but Ultima, with Antonio's help, is able to banish the curse. Antonio realizes that there is no way to explain Ultima's powers within the worldview of the Catholic church.

Antonio goes to visit the garden of Narciso, the town drunk. Afterward, they go to see the golden carp. Antonio's friend Cico tells him that only true believers can see the carp. Cico says that if the people cannot stop sinning, the carp will flood the land to rid it of humanity's evil. Antonio wishes sadly that there were a god of forgiveness. He idolizes the Virgin Mary because of the ideal of forgiveness that she represents.

One afternoon, Antonio witnesses an altercation between Narciso and Tenorio, the father of the wicked sisters who cursed Lucas. In a raging blizzard, Tenorio, who blames Ultima for the death of one of his daughters, goes out to kill the old woman. Narciso tries to stop him, and in front of Antonio, Tenorio shoots and kills Narciso. Antonio comes down with a high fever and has frightening and symbolic dreams.

At last, the time comes for Antonio to begin preparing for his Communion. But he seems to be surrounded by dissenting voices—that of his father, who seems to worship the earth more than he does the Christian God, and that of his friend Florence, who incisively points out the failings in Catholic thought. When Antonio finally takes Communion on Easter Sunday, he feels no different than he felt before. He still does not understand how there could be evil in the world or what kind of forgiveness is possible in a world of sin.

Ultima continues to teach Antonio lessons about moral independence and goodness. He goes with her to dispel the ghosts in a haunted house, and they discover that Tenorio has caused the haunting in order to take revenge on the man who owns the house. Ultima drives away the ghosts, but when the second of Tenorio's daughters falls ill, he begins to regard Ultima with even more hatred. Not long after that, Florence drowns while swimming in the river. Ultima sends Antonio to stay with his uncles to recover from the shock, and he spends a happy summer with them, learning how to tend a farm. On the journey there, Antonio and Gabriel talk about some of the questions that have been bothering Antonio, and Gabriel tells him that he will end the conflict between the Márezes and the Lunas and let Antonio choose his own destiny.

As Antonio makes his way from his uncles' fields to his grandfather's house one day toward the end of the summer, a murderous Tenorio chases after him. Antonio escapes, but Tenorio shoots Ultima's owl. When the owl dies, Ultima is doomed to die as well because the owl is her spiritual familiar, or guardian. Antonio sits with her at her bedside and buries the owl as she requests after she dies.

CHARACTER LIST

Antonio Márez The precocious protagonist of *Bless Me, Ultima*, Antonio is six years old at the beginning of the novel. Antonio is serious, thoughtful, and prone to moral questioning, and his experiences force him to confront difficult issues that blur the lines between right and wrong. He turns to both pagan and Christian ideologies for guidance, but he doubts both traditions. With Ultima's help, Antonio makes the transition from childhood to adolescence and begins to make his own choices and to accept responsibility for their consequences.

Gabriel and María Márez Antonio's parents, whose frequently conflicting views make it difficult for Antonio to accept either of their belief systems. María, the devoutly Catholic daughter of a farmer, wants Antonio to follow her Luna family tradition by becoming a priest. Gabriel is the son of vaqueros, or cowboys, and he prefers that Antonio follow the Márez tradition of restless wandering across the llano, or plains. Both parents love and revere Ultima.

Ultima An elderly curandera, a healer endowed with the spiritual power of her ancestors. Ultima is a wise, complex, mysterious character. Ultima's power is often misunderstood and feared by the community. Many people refer to her as a bruja, or witch. Even Antonio is confused about the moral nature of Ultima's power— no one knows if she is truly a witch. Ultima is a firm believer in tolerance and understanding, however, and she teaches Antonio that different belief systems can offer equally valid ways of understanding the world.

Narciso   The town drunk. Narciso is good friends with Gabriel because they both share a deep and passionate love for the llano. Narciso demonstrates a strong appreciation for the richness of the earth—his garden is a lush masterpiece full of sweet vegetables and fruits. Narciso respects and loves Ultima deeply. Tenorio kills him because he supports Ultima.

Tenorio Trementina and his three daughters   Tenorio is a malicious saloon-keeper and barber in El Puerto. His three daughters perform a black mass and place a curse on Lucas Luna. Tenorio detests Ultima because she lifts the curse on Lucas. Soon after she does so, one of Tenorio's daughters dies. Hot-tempered and vengeful, Tenorio spends the rest of the novel plotting Ultima's death, which he finally achieves by killing her owl familiar, her spiritual guardian.

Cico   One of Antonio's closer friends. Unlike most of Antonio's friends, he is quiet and gentle. Cico exposes Antonio to yet another belief system when he takes Antonio to see the golden carp, a pagan god who lives in the river.

Florence   One of Antonio's friends. Although Florence does not believe in God, he attends catechism to be with his friends. Florence's active, vocal questioning of Catholic orthodoxy is partly a result of his own difficult past; both of Florence's parents are dead, and his sisters have become prostitutes. Florence shows Antonio that the Catholic Church is not perfect and that religion can fail.

Antonio's friends: Abel, Bones, Ernie, Horse, Lloyd, Red, and the Vitamin Kid   An exuberant group of boys who frequently curse and fight. Horse loves to wrestle, but everyone fears Bones more because he is reckless and perhaps even crazy. Ernie is a braggart who frequently teases Antonio. The Vitamin Kid is the fastest runner in Guadalupe. Red is a Protestant, so he is often teased by the other boys. Lloyd enjoys reminding everyone that they can be sued for even the most minor offenses. Abel, the smallest boy in the group, frequently urinates in inappropriate places.

Lupito A war veteran who has been deeply mentally affected by the war. After Lupito murders Chávez's brother, the local sheriff, in one of his deranged moments, Lupito is killed by a mob in front of young Antonio. Lupito's death provides the impetus for Antonio's serious moral and religious questioning.

Andrew, Eugene, and León Márez Antonio's older brothers. For most of Antonio's childhood, his brothers are fighting in World War II. When they return home, they suffer post-traumatic stress as a result of the war. Restless and depressed, they all eventually leave home to pursue independent lives, crushing Gabriel's dream of moving his family to California.

Deborah and Theresa Márez Antonio's older sisters. Most of the time, they play with dolls and speak English, a language Antonio does not begin to learn until he attends school.

Antonio's uncles: Juan, Lucas, Mateo, and Pedro Luna María's brothers are farmers. They struggle with Gabriel to lay a claim to Antonio's future. They want him to become a farmer or a priest, but Gabriel wants Antonio to be a vaquero in the Márez tradition. Antonio's uncles are quiet and gentle, and they plant their crops by the cycle of the moon.

Father Byrnes A Catholic priest who gives catechism lessons to Antonio and his friends. He is a stern priest with hypocritical and unfair policies. He punishes Florence for the smallest offenses because Florence challenges the Catholic orthodoxy, but he fails to notice, and perhaps even ignores, the misbehavior of the other boys. Rather than teach the children to understand God, he prefers to teach them to fear God.

Chávez   Chávez is the father of Antonio's friend Jasón. He leads a mob to find Lupito after Lupito kills Chávez's brother, the local sheriff. He forbids Jasón to visit an Indian who lives near the town, but Jasón disobeys him.

Jasón Chávez   One of Antonio's friends. He disobeys his father when he continues to visit an Indian who lives near the town, but Jasón disobeys him.

Jasón Chávez's Indian   A friend of Jasón's who is disliked by Jasón's father. Cico tells Antonio that the story of the golden carp originally comes from the Indian.

Prudencio Luna   The father of María and her brothers. He is a quiet man who prefers not to become involved in other peoples' conflicts. When Tenorio declares an all out war against Ultima, he does not want his sons to get involved, even though Ultima saved Lucas's life.

Miss Maestas   Antonio's first-grade teacher. Although Antonio does not speak English well, Miss Maestas recognizes his bright spark of intelligence. Under her tutelage, Antonio unlocks the secrets of words. She promotes him to the third grade at the end of the year.

Rosie   The woman who runs the local brothel. Antonio has a deep fear of the brothel because it represents sin. He is devastated when he finds out that his brother Andrew frequents it.

Samuel   One of Antonio's closer friends. He is also the Vitamin Kid's brother. Unlike most of Antonio's friends, Samuel is gentle and quiet. He tells Antonio about the golden carp.

Téllez   One of Gabriel's friends. He challenges Tenorio when Tenorio speaks badly of Ultima. Not long afterward, a curse is laid on his home. Ultima agrees to lift the curse, explaining that Téllez's grandfather once hanged three Comanche Indians for raiding his flocks. Ultima performs a Comanche funeral ceremony on Téllez's land, and ghosts cease to haunt his home.

Ultima's teacher   Ultima's teacher was also known as el hombre volador, or "the flying man." He gave her the owl that became her spirit familiar, her guardian. He told her to do good works with her powers but to avoid interfering with a person's destiny. The invocation of his name inspires awe and respect among the people who have heard about his legendary powers.

Miss Violet   Antonio's third-grade teacher. She does not speak Spanish.

ANALYSIS OF MAJOR CHARACTERS

ANTONIO

In *Bless Me, Ultima,* Antonio leaves his childhood behind and seeks to reconcile his conflicting cultural and religious identities. Although Antonio is only six years old at the start of the narrative, he already possesses a keenly questioning mind, a great deal of moral curiosity, and a solemn appreciation for the seriousness of life. Some of his traits are typical of children his age, such as his anxiety at leaving his mother to start school. In other ways, Antonio is extraordinary. He is much more serious than other children, particularly compared to his rowdy and vulgar group of young friends. He is also acutely sensitive to his ambiguous place in the world, as he is trapped between two competing cultural visions. His father is a vaquero who wants Antonio to ride the llano and appreciate the open prairie; his mother is a daughter of farmers who wants Antonio to become a priest. Antonio is deeply troubled about his own uncertain destiny, but Ultima, a folk healer, guides him in his efforts to understand the world.

After Antonio witnesses the death of Lupito, one of the town's residents, his moral searching becomes even more intense, as he suddenly plunges into a crisis of faith. He becomes unsure for the first time about the validity of the Catholic faith. His intense desire to know the truth, one of the major components of his character, leads him into a spiral of questioning and uncertainty regarding sin, innocence, death, the afterlife, forgiveness, and the nature of God. For the rest of the novel, Antonio develops from childhood to maturity, as Ultima teaches him to make his own moral choices, to live in harmony with nature, to draw from all the traditions available to him, and to refrain from judging others when their beliefs differ from his own.

Ultima's guidance leads Antonio to resolve many of the conflicts within and around him. He realizes that he can determine his future and that he alone will decide what he becomes. Though the novel is narrated by the adult Antonio looking back over his childhood, we never learn what Antonio does decide to do with his life, whether he becomes a priest, a vaquero or something entirely different. Ultima remarks sadly to María that Antonio's destiny is to become "a man of learning," and in the most general sense, this idea is probably more important than the question of Antonio's career. Antonio is a man of learning because he understands that his experiences are lessons about life and because he knows that he must take life's lessons to heart, even when they are difficult, painful, or disappointing.

ULTIMA

The old healer Ultima lives and teaches the moral system that the novel espouses. Antonio's relationship with Ultima is the most important bond in the novel. Ultima acts as Antonio's mentor and helps him cope with his anxieties and uncertainties. Ultima claims a spiritual connection to Antonio that manifests its power in Chapter 1, when Antonio dreams of Ultima burying his afterbirth to keep his destiny secret from the arguing families of his parents. By presenting herself as the keeper of his destiny, Ultima immediately establishes a central role in Antonio's psyche. Ultima uses her unique position of influence with benevolence, preferring to teach Antonio to think for himself rather than indoctrinating him with her own sense of morality.

Like Antonio, Ultima is grounded in both the indigenous and Catholic traditions. She understands that life and spirituality can be viewed in many different and equally valid ways. Although the Catholic church does not recognize her mystical powers, Ultima respects the wisdom of the Catholic faith and attends mass regularly. Her appreciation for multiple faiths and perspectives bolsters her conviction that each person must make independent moral decisions, rather than blindly trust any single authority. Ultima tries to instill in Antonio the same tolerance, independence, and open-mindedness that define her faith and outlook. This view compels Ultima to treat Antonio with understanding and respect, even when he is a small and obedient child. Rather than force Antonio to help her with Lucas's exorcism, for instance, Ultima clearly explains what is at stake and allows Antonio to make his own decision. At the end of the novel, on her deathbed, Ultima treats Antonio as her spiritual heir, asking him to bury the owl that has symbolized her life force throughout the book. Though Ultima dies, her spirit and her influence will guide Antonio throughout his life.

GABRIEL

At first glance, Gabriel appears to be a washed-up old vaquero, or cowboy, who lives in a state of nostalgic regret on a patch of barren land. Gabriel works a demeaning job, drinks himself into a stupor on a weekly basis, and frequently fights with his wife. But as the novel progresses, the depth and dignity of Gabriel's relationship with the llano becomes clear. Even though he lives in a state of regret, he does so only out of his genuine fondness for the vaquero way of life. His choice to live on barren rather than fertile land results from his desire to be near the llano. His barren surroundings also support the idea that his family lives on the threshold of civilization and isolation.

The family's in-between state causes a great deal of conflict between Gabriel and his wife, María, a Catholic who would like to live in a civilized town. For the sake of María and his family, Gabriel leaves the llano, moves to town, and begins to attend church. Gabriel continually demonstrates maturity, equanimity, and self-sacrifice in this vein as the story progresses. María tries to force Antonio to follow her family's tradition and become a priest, but Gabriel does not coax him to follow his background and become a vaquero. Instead, Gabriel wants Antonio to become a vaquero only if he chooses that lifestyle. At the conclusion of the novel, Gabriel volunteers to put aside the conflict with the Lunas and help Antonio make his own choice about his future. Like Antonio himself, Gabriel has a serious and inquisitive mind. He has suffered hardship and bad luck, but he continues to strive to do the right thing and to help the people he loves.

CHARACTER ANALYSIS

THEMES, MOTIFS & SYMBOLS

THEMES

Themes are the fundamental and often universal ideas explored in a literary work.

THE IMPORTANCE OF MORAL INDEPENDENCE

An emphasis on thinking independently about moral decisions pervades *Bless Me, Ultima*. Antonio's progress toward moral independence is the main marker of his maturity and development throughout the novel. Antonio's struggle to reconcile the complexities of his experience with his religion leads him to conclude that he must make his own decisions. He becomes increasingly frustrated by the failure of the church to explain the most pressing questions about morality and human experience.

Ultima acts as Antonio's guide as he learns the importance of moral independence. Ultima teaches him that the most difficult questions about life can never be answered entirely by a single religion or cultural tradition. Antonio has questions about evil, forgiveness, truth, and the soul, questions he can answer only for himself. Antonio once believed that the Communion ritual would answer all his questions, but Ultima teaches him that he must think for himself and arrive at his own conclusions.

THE INFLUENCE OF CULTURE ON IDENTITY

Bless Me, Ultima explores the difficulty of reconciling conflicting cultural traditions. In the end, Anaya suggests that a person can draw from several cultural traditions to forge a more complex and adaptable identity. Antonio is so eager to find a single, definitive answer to the questions that haunt him because he has been influenced by many conflicting cultures. The first major conflict involves his parents. His Luna mother wishes for him to become a priest, while his vaquero father wishes for him to ride the llano. Each parent has deeply rooted cultural convictions. Next is the conflict within his town between its Spanish and indigenous cultures. We see evidence of this conflict in the pronounced tension between Ultima's mystical folklore and the Catholic church. Another conflict takes place at Antonio's school between Spanish and English speakers.

Anaya uses these conflicts to explore the influence of culture on identity. Many characters in the book are limited by their cultural prejudices and never learn to look beyond their own assumptions. For example, the townspeople condemn Narciso for being a drunk and refuse to acknowledge that his traumatic experience in the war might play a part in his psychological state. Ultima teaches Antonio to avoid the limitations inherent in abiding by one culture, one religion, or one creed. Instead, Ultima encourages Antonio to embrace all of the cultural influences in his life to become a better person.

MOTIFS

Motifs are recurring structures, contrasts, or literary devices that can help to develop and inform the text's major themes.

DREAMS

Antonio has a number of dreams throughout the novel, from his early dream about watching his own birth to his later dreams about his brothers calling for his help. Anaya uses the recurrent dream motif to show how Antonio's interpretations of his thoughts and experiences change as he develops as a character. In his early dreams, for instance, Antonio is largely preoccupied with the question of his destiny, of whether he will become a vaquero or a priest. But in his later dreams, he is preoccupied with much larger questions of family, morality, and duty. This gradual transformation, traced in dreams, reflects Antonio's growth from childhood to maturity. His dreams also offer him a rich and variable set of images and symbols with which to understand his own life.

FAMILY

The recurring presence of various family relationships—uncles, siblings, and parents, especially—provides a subtle commentary on the nature of identity and ultimately underscores the book's main theme of moral independence. Many of Antonio's family members seek to define his future, especially his uncles, who argue about whether he will become a priest or a vaquero. Antonio looks to other members of his family to help define his identity, especially when he tries to model himself after Andrew, his older brother. In the end, Antonio must learn to make his own choices, drawing from the wisdom and experience of his family, but not being limited by their wishes and perspectives.

LEARNING AND EDUCATION

Ultima once predicts vaguely that Antonio will be a "man of learning." Many scenes in the book explore Antonio's education, both religious (his Communion classes) and academic (his school classes). Antonio's growth and development serve as examples of education. Ultima believes that every experience helps inform one's identity and perspective on life. *Bless Me, Ultima* is the story of Antonio's growth from childhood to maturity. His progress is represented by his gradually expanding education, both in the classroom and in his own introspective interpretation of his experience.

TOLERANCE AND UNDERSTANDING

Ultima represents the importance of tolerance and understanding. Though she comes from an indigenous mystical tradition, she openly acknowledges the value of the Catholic faith. She also encourages Antonio to draw from the various conflicting sets of ideals that define his outlook. Learning the importance of tolerance marks Antonio's growth, especially as he begins to realize that some religions may be better suited to some people than to others, as Florence is seemingly better suited to the faith of the golden carp than to Catholicism.

SYMBOLS

Symbols are objects, characters, figures, or colors used to represent abstract ideas or concepts.

THE GOLDEN CARP

The golden carp represents a magical religious order not connected to Catholicism. The golden carp legend offers its own brand of wisdom, comfort, and moral guidance. Within the context of the novel's themes, the carp supports the idea that every religious tradition offers different, but equally valid, lessons about the world. Antonio first rejects the golden carp, feeling that he is abandoning God by simply pursuing an interest in the magical fish. He learns later that the carp can actually help in his endeavor to draw from all the cultural and religious sources available to him in crafting his own identity and finding his own answers.

ULTIMA'S OWL
Ultima's owl represents her life force and the power of her religious mysticism. The owl sings softly outside Antonio's window at night. Its song symbolizes Ultima's comforting presence in Antonio's life and the protective power of her magic. At the end of the novel, Tenorio's killing of the owl literally destroys Ultima's life force and leads very quickly to her death. Antonio equates Ultima with the owl—when he buries it, he says that he is really burying Ultima.

THE VIRGIN OF GUADALUPE
María's statue of the Virgin of Guadalupe symbolizes forgiveness, understanding, and the resolution of cultural conflict. The story of the dark-skinned Virgin represents the reconciliation of the European Catholic Church with the indigenous culture of Antonio's homeland. Antonio turns to the Virgin repeatedly when he is frustrated by his failure to find a forgiving god.

Summary & Analysis

Uno (1)

Writing as an adult, Antonio Márez recounts events that occur when he was six years old. Ultima, an elderly curandera, or healer, comes to live with his family. The night before Ultima's arrival, Antonio lies in his bed in the little attic above his mother's kitchen. He hears his parents talking about Ultima. His father, Gabriel, says that Ultima is old, and though she has served the people as a healer her entire life, she has now been reduced to living alone out on the llano, the great New Mexico grassland near Antonio's home. Antonio knows that his father is a vaquero, a cowboy, and loves the wildness of the llano, while his mother, María, is from the Luna family, who are all farmers, and prefers civilization. Long ago, María convinced Gabriel to move to the town of Guadalupe so that their children could have an education, and Gabriel still misses the life on the open plains of the llano.

Antonio is happy that his parents have decided to take Ultima into their home and to provide for her. As he drifts off into sleep, he has a dream in which he floats over the hills of the llano to the village of Las Pasturas and toward the window of a lighted hut. There, a woman is in labor, and Antonio recognizes that he is witnessing his own birth. After the baby Antonio is born, his mother's brothers arrive and declare that he will be a Luna and perhaps become a priest. His father's brothers declare that he will continue their tradition of restless wandering on the llano. Each family wishes to dispose of the afterbirth according to their family traditions: the Lunas seek to bury it in the earth, while the vaqueros seek to burn it and scatter the ashes across the open plains. Ultima halts the ensuing disagreement by stating that she will bury the afterbirth herself. She declares that only she will know Antonio's destiny.

Antonio is anxious the next morning. He knows that he will soon begin school, and he is nervous at the thought of leaving his mother. He talks with his mother about his birth; she confirms that Ultima helped at her bedside, and she urges her children to treat Ultima with respect when the elderly woman arrives. She then strongly implies that she wants Antonio to become a priest. Troubled, Antonio decides to visit his friend Jasón but finds that he is not home. Antonio surmises that Jasón has defied his father's wishes by going to visit an Indian who lives alone in the hills. Antonio returns home to work in the garden.

Later that day, Gabriel arrives with Ultima. When Antonio shakes Ultima's hand, he senses the power of a whirlwind pass around him. He calls her by her given name instead of the customary salutation, Grande, and Ultima says that she knew when he was born that she would one day be close to him. Ultima's owl takes up residence near Antonio's home. Although owls are said to be a disguise taken by brujas, or witches, Antonio dreams that the owl carries the Virgin of Guadalupe and all the babes of Limbo to heaven.

ANALYSIS

From the beginning of the novel, Anaya links Antonio's anxieties about change in his life to the culture in which he lives. Ultima's entrance into Antonio's life marks a stressful time of change for Antonio. Anaya emphasizes Antonio's position on the threshold of change by portraying his nervousness about beginning school, separating from his mother, and facing his uncertain future. Because of the conflicted nature of his parents' marriage, Antonio is essentially caught between two competing cultures, each of which carries its own set of expectations and assumptions. The vaquero lifestyle favored by his father emphasizes the values of independence, freedom, and mobility, all of which are manifest in the vaqueros' love of the llano. The Luna family lifestyle favored by Antonio's mother, on the other hand, emphasizes stability, productivity, and family, which manifest themselves in the Lunas' desire to fence the llano and build towns. Even though Antonio is only six years old, his future already hangs between these two contrasting alternatives, and Antonio's dream about his birth reveals the anxiety this pressure causes him. Ultima's declaration that she is the one who knows Antonio's destiny foreshadows Ultima's role as Antonio's guide in the process of reconciling his heritages and building a future out of both.

Ultima's role as a curandera demonstrates the extent to which Chicano culture is a mixture of multiple, and often conflicting, influences. Curanderismo is the practice of folk medicine, a healing art heavily influenced by the knowledge and ancient religions of indigenous peoples. Curanderismo is associated with the treatment of both physical and supernatural illnesses. When Spanish Catholics arrived in the New World, they regarded curanderismo as a form of witchcraft and often killed those who practiced it. However, over the course of time, the intermixing between Spaniards and native people produced a mixed religious culture. In Antonio's small town, curanderismo exists side by side with Catholicism and often in harmony with it. Anaya also illustrates this blend of religious belief in the portrayal of Antonio's mother, María, who is a devout Catholic and yet respects and even reveres Ultima's powers.

Antonio's inherent trust of the old woman underscores Anaya's implication that the Catholic Church cannot explain certain kinds of power, especially Ultima's. The practitioners of curanderismo are still regarded with suspicion by many, a distrust that reveals a lingering conflict between European and indigenous religious practices. Antonio's trust in her goodness reveals that Antonio is on his way to independent decision-making, because he can reconcile conflicting belief systems.

Antonio's feeling of conflict results from the demands placed upon him to reconcile his parents' radically different heritages. His attempt to do so forms the main discussion of the novel. María and her family have a profoundly spiritual relationship with the earth, which is symbolized by their desire to bury Antonio's afterbirth in the ground. Their hope that Antonio will become a priest attests to their devout Catholic faith. The mystical character of their relationship to the earth is deeply tied to indigenous spirituality, while their devotion to Catholicism represents the extent to which European culture has shaped them. Despite the violent clash between Spanish and indigenous religions, a culture that contains harmonious elements of both has survived.

Gabriel's family lives the vaquero, or cowboy, way of life. They are driven by the same adventurous, restless spirit that drove the Spaniards across the ocean to the New World, as their name, derived from the Spanish word for ocean, implies. They are also superb horsemen. However, Gabriel's reverence for Ultima shows that his worldview is heavily influenced by indigenous culture. Like the Luna family, he has a spiritual and mystical relationship with the land, but he expresses it in a different manner. His love of the open llano is just as spiritual as the Lunas' love of their farmland, but it embodies an incompatible view of the world. He cannot easily adapt to the slow and stable life of towns and farms, as we see in Gabriel's general antipathy toward life in Guadalupe and in his deep nostalgia for life on the open plains.

DOS (2)

SUMMARY
The whole family is glad that Ultima has come to stay with them. María is happy to have a woman to talk to, and Antonio's two older sisters are happy to have someone to help with their chores so that they can spend more time playing together with dolls. Gabriel talks to Ultima about his desire to move to California, a wish he now feels will never come true because his older sons are fighting in World War II, and he cannot move his young family alone.

Antonio is happy because he and Ultima quickly become friends. Ultima takes Antonio on walks to gather herbs and teaches him about their healing properties. Antonio says that he begins to hear the voice of the river. He senses that his family's peaceful isolation is about to end. Jasón's father, Chávez, comes to the Márez home shouting that Lupito, a local war veteran, shot Chávez's brother, the sheriff, dead. When Gabriel joins Chávez and the other men searching for Lupito, Antonio secretly follows them to the river. He sees Lupito, armed with a pistol, hidden in the water. Antonio makes a small noise, and Lupito looks down at him. But just then, the searchlights fall on Lupito, and he is confronted by his pursuers. Lupito runs off again into the reeds, out of sight of the men on the bridge. Gabriel and Narciso, the town drunk, try to explain to the mob that Lupito is shell-shocked because of the war, but after crying out something about Japanese soldiers, Lupito shoots his pistol into the air, drawing the fire of his pursuers. Lupito begs Antonio for his blessing as he dies.

Antonio runs home, sobbing and reciting the Act of Contrition, the last prayer that Catholics say before dying. When he realizes that Ultima's owl has been with him the whole time, he loses his fear. He fears that the river will be stained with blood forever. He thinks about the town, which he knows his father despises, and the llano, and he wonders why Lupito had to die. He remembers when his father built their house. Rather than choosing to build on a patch of fertile ground, Gabriel built a house on a barren place at the start of the llano. Antonio enters the house and Ultima meets him. She cleans him and puts him to bed. Ultima explains that it is not for them to judge whether Lupito or the men who killed him will go to hell. Antonio dreams of his three older brothers discussing their father's dream to build a castle in the hills. When Antonio states that they must gather around their father, they reply that he is supposed to fulfill María's dream and become a priest. When they try to cross the River of the Carp to build Gabriel's castle, a mournful voice calls Antonio's name. His brothers shrink in fear, saying that it is La Llorona, the "Weeping Woman," or Lupito asking for his blessing. Antonio declares that it is the presence of the river. He calms it so that his brothers can cross.

ANALYSIS

Antonio's changing attitude toward nature reflects the ways in which he is developing into an independent and thoughtful young boy. As a child, Antonio's fear of the llano represents his dependence on his family and his youth. Later, Ultima helps him appreciate the natural beauty of the wide plains that his father loves so much. Her guidance allows Antonio to find harmony between his conflicting paternal and maternal heritages. This development foreshadows Antonio's ultimately optimistic end, but it also suggests a new period of difficulty and conflict that parallels his general transition away from childish innocence and toward a more adult wisdom. After he witnesses Lupito's death, Antonio becomes preoccupied with sin, punishment, and the loss of innocence. Antonio's confrontation with ideas of good and evil manifests itself in his use of religion to try to understand the world. Antonio recites the Act of Contrition as he runs home, even though he doesn't fully understand its significance. Furthermore, Lupito forces Antonio to take the figurative role of priest when Lupito asks Antonio for a blessing. Antonio must suddenly deal with the moral significance of an adult dilemma.

Antonio's dream about his brothers further symbolizes the conflict between his maternal and paternal heritages. But unlike his brothers, Antonio now senses that there is greater strength in embracing his entire heritage than in choosing any one part of it. The novel suggests that Antonio's maternal and paternal heritages result from the same conflict, the conflict between Spanish and indigenous cultures. Antonio's struggle to reconcile his family heritage is much like the struggle to evaluate the influences of the varying cultures of New Mexico.

Anaya's reference to the legend of La Llorona demonstrates how *Bless Me, Ultima* breaks from a traditional Western canon of great works. Like the more commonly known legend of Medea, La Llorona is the story of a woman who kills her children in a fit of rage.

However, the legend of La Llorona is more relevant within Antonio's culture as an illustration of his continuing fear of veering from his parents' expectations. The legend of La Llorona is a classic of Mexican and Chicano folklore. Some versions of the tale suggest that La Llorona kills her children because their father leaves her or makes her jealous of her children. Many versions of the legend suggest that she died or killed herself when she realized what she had done. Her spirit wanders the river, crying out for her lost children.

Many versions of the tale associate La Llorona with evil. Some versions describe her visits to lustful young men whom she lures to their deaths. Other versions describe her efforts to steal living children who are out by the river late at night, mistaking them for her own dead children. Because some versions imply that the children are disobeying their parents, parents often use the story to frighten children into obedience. In some versions, however, La Llorona is a sympathetic figure deserving of pity. In others, she is a malevolent force to be feared. Gabriel and Narciso ask the mob to have mercy on Lupito because he was mad when he killed the sheriff. The connection is that Lupito and La Llorona were both insane when they murdered, and thus they cannot be held accountable to rational moral judgment.

The pairing of La Llorona and Lupito in Antonio's dream shows that he is beginning to deal with morally ambivalent issues. Antonio wants to make moral sense out of Lupito's death, but easy answers elude him. The figure of La Llorona expresses Antonio's anxieties about growing up, about disobeying his parents, and about wandering by the river. His dream ends with the voice of María mourning that her son is growing older, an apparition that phrases Antonio's anxiety about leaving his mother in her own voice. Antonio is developing an independent self-consciousness and learning to combine elements of both his parents' heritages. As a young boy, though, he is still ambivalent about the consequences of change.

TRES (3)

SUMMARY
When Antonio wakes, he ponders the fate of Lupito's soul and those of the men who killed him. He thinks that, according to Catholic principles, Lupito must be in hell because Lupito died having committed a mortal sin. He hopes that God will forgive Lupito, but he

thinks sadly that God does not forgive anyone. He wonders whether the water of the river will carry Lupito's soul away.

Antonio lies in bed and listens to his parents quarrel. Their frequent Sunday morning arguments about religion are a result of Gabriel's Saturday night drinking. María is a devout Catholic, but Gabriel's vaquero mindset causes him to distrust priests because to him they stand for order and civilization. Antonio knows that Gabriel's father once dragged a priest from church and beat him after the priest preached against something that Antonio's grandfather had done. At last Antonio goes downstairs, and María scolds Antonio for not being properly formal when greeting Ultima. Ultima requests that María not scold Antonio, as the night was hard on all the men in town. María protests that Antonio is still a baby. She says that she thinks it is a sin for boys to become men. Gabriel hotly declares that it is not a sin, only the way of the world, and María argues that life corrupts the innocence and purity that God bequeaths to children. She says bitterly that if Antonio becomes a priest, he will be spared from the corruption of life. Gabriel pours coffee for Ultima, and Antonio realizes with some surprise that Gabriel and Ultima are the only grown-ups he knows who eat or drink before taking Communion on Sundays.

Many women in town are dressed in mourning because they have lost sons and husbands in the war. Antonio notes that the war has indirectly claimed two more victims: Chávez's brother and Lupito. Antonio lingers near his mother, who smoothes his hair, and he feels soothed by her presence. He feels another jolt of anxiety when he realizes again that when he starts school soon, he will have to leave her. Antonio and Ultima discuss the events of the previous night. Antonio asks Ultima how his father can take Communion if he committed the sin of firing at Lupito. Ultima replies that she doesn't think Gabriel fired at Lupito, but she warns that no one should presume to decide whom God does and does not forgive. On the way to the church, the family passes a brothel situated in a ramshackle mansion that belongs to a woman named Rosie. María makes her children bow their heads as they pass, and Antonio realizes that Rosie is evil, but evil in a different way from a witch. Before mass, Antonio mingles with the other boys. As they play, they discuss the night's events. One of the boys brags that his father saw Lupito kill the sheriff. Antonio says nothing about Lupito's death.

ANALYSIS

Antonio's thoughts and actions in this chapter indicate a new obsession with sin and punishment. Ultima acts as a mentor to Antonio, guiding his inexperienced mind through new adult terrain. For example, her explanation that the men of the llano will not kill without reason is an attempt to address Antonio's curiosity regarding the morality of murder. Ultima also tries to teach Antonio a larger moral lesson regarding salvation and damnation. Her suggestion that people must make independent moral decisions but should not make decisions regarding salvation and damnation introduces into the novel the idea that morality is not absolute. Ultima uses Catholic terms in her explanations to Antonio because Antonio is trying to make sense of Lupito's death within a Catholic framework.

One sign that Antonio is leaving his childhood behind is his realization that the grown-ups he loves and trusts can make mistakes. Narciso and Gabriel's failed attempt to save Lupito, as well as the triumph of Chavez's and the others' blind anger and fear, forces Antonio to confront the fact that good intentions and good actions do not always achieve their desired results. As Antonio's mentor, Ultima does not tell him what to think; rather, she tells him how people like his father and Narciso make moral decisions. Her approach gives Antonio the freedom to apply his understanding to his own decisions. Ultima's style of teaching implies that she is more interested in helping Antonio develop into an independent person than in teaching him any particular moral outlook on life.

María's and Gabriel's opinions regarding the transition between childhood and adolescence are based on the issues of sin and punishment that preoccupy Antonio. His mother associates growing up with learning how to sin, while Gabriel and Ultima view growing up as an inevitable process that is not good or bad in itself. María's worldview results from a primarily religious outlook on life, but Gabriel and Ultima's embodies a natural outlook. As a boy becomes a man, he uses his experiences and his knowledge to make decisions. The pressures that accompany each of these outlooks flare up when the subject of Antonio's future comes up yet again. María's religiosity leads her to the conclusion that the only hope for Antonio's salvation lies in his becoming a priest, while Gabriel's love of independence causes him to insist that no one but Antonio should decide whether he becomes a priest. His response reveals both his belief that meddling in another's destiny is wrong and his aversion for priests. María, as a staunch Catholic, supports meddling in

Antonio's future as much as possible because the state of his soul is at stake. She also fears Antonio's inevitable maturation for precisely the reasons that Ultima seeks to guide him: because he will start making his own decisions soon and will no longer constantly look to her for guidance.

CUATRO (4)

SUMMARY

As the summer comes to an end, Antonio spends his mornings walking with Ultima, gathering herbs and medicines from the llano. During this happy time, Antonio grows to love both the llano and the river. Ultima teaches him that plants have spirits like people and tells him stories about the old days. Antonio realizes that Ultima is happiest when she is out on the llano, and her happiness helps him to realize that he too is a part of the llano and a part of nature. Antonio tells Ultima that he will soon visit his mother's brothers, and Ultima tells him that she is an old friend of his mother's father. He asks her why his Luna relatives are so quiet, and she replies that it is in the Luna blood to be quiet like the moon, just as it is in the Márez blood to be loud and restless like the sea. (In Spanish, la luna means "moon" and el mar means "sea.") Antonio feels the presence of the river and wonders again about Lupito's soul.

Back at home, Antonio and Ultima dry the plants on the chicken shed. María tells them over dinner that, as Antonio had expected, it will soon be time to visit the Lunas to help with the harvest, a yearly ritual that keeps Antonio close to his grandfather and uncles. Antonio spends the rest of the afternoon playing at Jáson's house and then cuts wild alfalfa by the river to feed to the rabbits.

Every night, Antonio's family prays before María's statue of the Virgin of Guadalupe, a beautiful, two-foot-tall likeness of the Virgin in a blue gown. Antonio loves her because she always forgives; the Virgin is his favorite saint. He knows that she is the patron saint of his land. On the foot of the statue a little paint has chipped away so that the white plaster is visible, and Antonio thinks of the plaster as the Virgin's pure soul.

That night, Antonio hears Ultima's owl singing its mournful song outside his attic window. Antonio slips into sleep and has a dream in which the Virgin speaks to María. The Virgin promises María that his older brothers will return home from the war safely. When María asks her to make Antonio a priest, Antonio sees the Virgin wearing the clothing of mourning for him while standing on the moon. When he cries out in his sleep, Ultima comes to comfort him.

ANALYSIS

Because Anaya's audience likely has had little previous experience with the culture he describes, Ultima is a mentor figure not only to Antonio, but also to us as readers as well. She relates both to Antonio and to the general reader cultural beliefs about the spirits of plants in nature and also historical information about Antonio's indigenous ancestors and about the Spanish in Europe. Ultima's guidance introduces Antonio to his cultural identity as a Chicano. The knowledge she conveys to him is particularly important not only because Antonio will be in school soon but also because of the changes his culture will face as it integrates with a modernized world. In particular, Ultima's advice that Antonio does not need to choose between his parents' conflicting wishes for him gives Antonio the resolve to move beyond his parents' split views. Ultima's lessons illustrate a deeper desire: she wants him to listen to the voices of the land and his heritage. She believes that this knowledge will help him build his future out of the pieces of his ancestral past.

Although María's devout Catholicism represents the Spanish elements in her cultural tradition, the form of Catholicism she practices is naturally a mixture of both Spanish and indigenous elements. The legend of the Virgin of Guadalupe is partly an allegory of the cultural and racial clash between Spanish colonists and indigenous peoples. When the Spanish came to the New World, they launched an intense campaign to convert indigenous people to Catholicism. The legend has it that the Virgin Mary appeared to a native man who was baptized with the Christian name Juan Diego. However, she appeared with the dark skin of the indigenous peoples of Mexico. She told Juan Diego that she wanted a church built on the hill of Tepeyac, the former location of an Aztec temple destroyed by the Spanish colonists.

The Virgin is the embodiment of both the novel's main forces of conflict and their inherent resolution; the Virgin both defines and heals the cultural struggle that preoccupies Antonio and his world, and she is thus a figure of extraordinary psychological importance in the book. Her story relates the original conflict between the indigenous peoples of Mexico and the Spanish colonists. Juan Diego, as a native man, had a great deal of difficulty getting an audience with the Spanish bishop. The bishop refused to believe Juan Diego's story. When the Virgin appeared to Juan Diego for the fourth time, she instructed him to pick some roses to take to the bishop as proof for his story. Juan Diego obeyed her. When he opened his cloak to spill the roses out in front of the bishop, the image of the dark-skinned Virgin Mary was emblazoned on his cloak. Thus the bishop constructed a small church on the hill; it was later replaced with a larger, more elaborate church, the Basilica. The dark-skinned Virgin Mary became known as the Virgin of Guadalupe, sometimes referred to as the Queen of Mexico. Representations of her image contain deep reds and blues, prominent colors in Mexican indigenous artwork.

Antonio's relationship to the Virgin of Guadalupe highlights his growing moral awareness. Before, he was largely concerned with sin and punishment. In this chapter, he begins to include forgiveness as an element of moral dilemmas. He views the Virgin of Guadalupe as the sweet, forgiving mediator between sinners and a wrathful, unforgiving God. His dream about the Virgin of Guadalupe reveals that he has begun to consider the possibility that he too can sin. He dreams that she prays in mourning over him, implying that she is asking God's forgiveness for him.

The dream also reveals Antonio's developing awareness of his own mortality. The dream has multiple meanings. It is possible that the Virgin is mourning his death. It is also possible that the dream means that becoming a priest does not save Antonio from sin as his mother wished. It could also mean that Antonio disappointed his mother's wishes by not becoming a priest. The dream symbolizes many of the conflicts that plague Antonio as he grows out of his childhood ignorance and innocence. It represents his preoccupation with sin and punishment and the possible significance of disobeying his mother's wishes for him. He is struggling to integrate his developing independence into a defined moral structure. The absence of a clear line between right and wrong in the dream illustrates Antonio's struggle with moral ambiguity. He is afraid of the inevitability that he will increasingly be subject to moral judgment as he grows older. However, he does not have to be alone while he makes the journey into the adult world of moral decision-making. Ultima is there to comfort him when he awakes.

On a subconscious level, Antonio relates to Ultima in the same way as he does to the Virgin. Throughout *Bless Me, Ultima*, Ultima is referred to as the mujer que no ha pecado, or "the woman who has not sinned." Antonio also had a dream that Ultima's owl flew the

Virgin to heaven. His parents frequently inspire the fear of punishment and judgment, but Ultima does not. Antonio reveals thoughts and feelings to her that he is not comfortable revealing to his parents, and in this way, she is the living embodiment of understanding and forgiveness, just as the Virgin is the iconic embodiment of understanding and forgiveness.

CINCO–NUEVE (5–9)

SUMMARY: CINCO (5)
Pedro Luna, Antonio's uncle, takes Antonio, his mother, his sisters, and Ultima to the Luna farms to help with the harvest. They stop first at the home of María's father, Prudencio Luna. Afterward, they settle into the home of one of María's brothers, Juan Luna, because it is his turn to host his sister and her children. Antonio overhears Juan urge María to send Antonio to them for a summer before Antonio is "lost" like his older brothers.

SUMMARY: SEIS (6)
That fall, Antonio begins school. When Ultima blesses him, he again feels a whirlwind sweeping around him. He recalls the evil whirlwinds on the llano, which he has been taught to ward off with the sign of the cross, and wonders why he feels the same whirlwind in Ultima's presence. Reflecting on this similarity, Antonio wonders if the powers of good and evil are the same. María presses Ultima to name Antonio's fate. Ultima replies sadly that Antonio will be "a man of learning." In his first day, Antonio learns to write his name, much to his teacher's pleasure. However, the class first laughs at him because he cannot speak English and because he eats green chili in tortillas for lunch. Feeling like an outcast, Antonio begins eating lunch with other children whose language and customs are different.

SUMMARY: SIETE (7)
The war ends, and Antonio dreams of three giants, his brothers. They ask for his "saving hand" because they are dying. Antonio wakes just in time to greet his brothers upon their return.

SUMMARY: OCHO (8)
Antonio's brothers spend the winter sleeping all day and spending their money on women and drink. All three of them suffer trauma from the war. Their parents say that they have "war-sickness." In

the spring, the brothers are restless to build their own independent lives, resisting Gabriel's urgings to follow his old dream of moving to California with them.

Summary: Nueve (9)

Antonio dreams that his three brothers urge him to enter Rosie's brothel. Antonio calls out that he must resist because he might become a priest. His brothers León and Eugene predict that he will eventually enter the brothel. Antonio begs Andrew to stay outside. Andrew promises not to enter until Antonio loses his innocence. Antonio hears the voices of a priest and María, who say that innocence lasts only until understanding. Antonio hears Ultima call out that his innocence is in the lonely llano. Antonio awakes to hear his brothers arguing with their parents. The brothers want to leave the family and strike out on their own. León and Eugene leave the next morning, but Andrew stays behind.

Andrew walks Antonio to school. The Vitamin Kid beats them in a race, calling Antonio a giant killer. At the end of the year, Antonio's teacher, Miss Maestas, promotes him from first to third grade. After school, Antonio goes fishing with Samuel, the Vitamin Kid's brother. Samuel asks if Antonio has ever fished for carp. Antonio replies that he hasn't because to do so is bad luck. Samuel tells Antonio a story that Jasón's Indian originally told. The story says that the gods sent the first people to the valley but forbade them to eat the carp. During a terrible drought, the people disobeyed the rule. One god pleaded for mercy, so the gods turned the people into carp instead of killing them. The god who saved the people grew sad, so he became a carp as well. However, he is larger than the other carp and golden in color. The story explains why eating carp is a sin. Samuel says that Cico, a local boy, will take Antonio to see the golden carp. When Antonio returns home, María is angry that he is so late. When she learns of his double promotion, however, she quickly forgets it.

Analysis: Cinco–Nueve (5–9)

Ultima's prediction that Antonio will be a "man of learning" shows that her conception of learning is broader than that of some of the other characters. Her prediction is not necessarily a confirmation that Antonio will fulfill María's hope that he become a priest. Her answer actually draws from a comment she makes earlier in the novel, when Antonio is trying to make sense of Lupito's death and

Ultima tells him that the ways of men are hard to learn. She seems to believe every man is a "man of learning" because acquiring life experiences is in itself a learning process. Ultima's sadness may simply result from her awareness that Antonio will face difficult times or from a sense that his mother may misinterpret her prediction.

Bless Me, Ultima is largely focused on the difficulty of reconciling cultural differences, and Antonio's entrance into school demonstrates one more way in which this difficulty pervades his life. There, he must address the conflict between Anglo and Chicano cultures, yet another set of identities for him to deal with along with the Spanish/indigenous and Luna/vaquero identities. Language plays a large role in his identity conflict at school, where his alienation is intense because he does not speak English. Anaya suggests, however, that even if he did, he would be unable to avoid confrontation with Anglo arrogance. Antonio struggles with his feelings of hurt and even resentment at his mother for sending him to school, another indication that Antonio is growing away from his childhood dependence on his mother. Coping with these feelings is basically the process of coping with change.

Antonio's dream in Chapter 7, in which his brothers are three giants who ask for his "saving hand," is open to many metaphorical interpretations, all of which address Antonio's gradual entrance into adolescence. The dream could mean that Antonio is reluctant to give up his innocent, childish idea that his brothers are infallible and unchanging. It could also mean that they are dying because they have changed too much to settle seamlessly into their old lives. When they do arrive, they are restless and aimless. Finally, León and Eugene decide to build independent lives elsewhere. The dream also reveals Antonio's awareness that the people he loves can sin despite his attempts to save them. Antonio also has difficulty coping with the idea that his brothers are men, not boys who will stay home with their mother.

Although Antonio loves to learn, his dream about the brothel reveals his anxiety about the morality of desiring knowledge. In this dream, he clearly associates knowledge of the flesh with sin. Antonio's refusal to enter the brothel on the grounds that he may someday want to become a priest results from his anxieties over whether not fulfilling his mother's wishes is immoral. In other words, he wonders if it is a sin not to fulfill her wishes. Anaya begins to link some of the thematic anxieties that have troubled the novel's characters from the beginning: growing up, becoming independent from one's parents, learning, and finding a clear moral framework in which to live one's life. Seen within the context of cultural identity, these concerns lie at the heart of *Bless Me, Ultima* and become increasingly pressing on Antonio as he grows older and is forced to make independent judgments more regularly.

At the same time that the novel intensifies its treatment of conflicting cultural identities, it begins to resolve Antonio's concern about growing older and leaving his mother. Although he spends much of the first several chapters of the book anxious about leaving his mother, once he actually arrives at school, Antonio solidifies his fragile new independence by forming relationships outside of his family. Some friends, like the Vitamin Kid, simply provide him with boyish fun. Others, like Samuel, are mentors as well as friends. Although Antonio suffers during the initial stages of developing a life independent of his mother, by the end of his first year of school, he begins to make decisions for himself. He demonstrates this self-awareness by choosing to go fishing with Samuel rather than returning home after school.

Once he has firmly acted on his new independence, he is ready to be exposed to an alternate religious view—the legend of the golden carp that Samuel tells him. The legend of the golden carp contains the same kind of moral themes contained in Catholic theology. The story involves sin, punishment, and forgiveness. Antonio's open mind allows him to realize that both religions represent different ways of making sense of the same issues of life, death, good, and evil. Just as Antonio realizes Catholicism's limits in understanding Ultima's power, he realizes that other religions are equally valid forms of knowledge about moral issues. Like Ultima's worldview, each religion simply provides a different set of principles and icons that people can use to understand the basic issues that define existence.

DIEZ–ONCE (10–11)

SUMMARY & ANALYSIS

SUMMARY: DIEZ (10)

The orange of the golden carp appeared at the edge of the pond. As he came out of the darkness of the pond the sun caught his shiny scales and the light reflected orange and yellow and red.

(See QUOTATIONS, *p. 55)*

When María's youngest brother, Lucas Luna, is near death that summer after having fallen ill the previous winter, neither a Las Vegas doctor nor the local priest can cure him. When Pedro, Lucas's brother, asks for Ultima's help, he explains that Lucas saw the daughters of Tenorio Trementina dancing the Black Mass, a blasphemous satanic ritual. When Lucas challenged them with a cross made from two sticks, they fled the scene. Within the week, Lucas fell ill.

Ultima says that she will need Antonio's help to cure Lucas. Antonio states that he will be proud to assist a curandera. As they approach El Puerto, they see the horned day moon, the moon of the Lunas, between two dark mesas at the end of the valley. When Ultima arrives in El Puerto, she forbids the Lunas to kill the coyotes that will surround Prudencio's home when she works her cure. When Ultima takes Antonio to confront Tenorio to warn him that his daughters must lift the curse or suffer the consequences, Tenorio makes the sign of the cross. Ultima declares that his daughters gathered Lucas's hair for their curse after he came to Tenorio for a haircut. Tenorio denies her accusations and calls her a bruja, or witch.

Ultima closes herself and Antonio in Lucas's room. After she forces a mixture of kerosene, water, and herbs down Lucas's throat, she asks Antonio if he is afraid, and Antonio says that he is not. She explains that the reason for his courage is that good is always stronger than evil. Antonio hears Ultima's owl attacking the coyotes surrounding Prudencio's home. Antonio enters a trance and finds that he cannot move or speak. When Lucas writhes in pain, Antonio feels pain as well. Ultima makes three clay dolls covered with wax and forces Lucas to take more medicine. Afterward, Antonio drifts to sleep. When he wakes, he vomits green bile. Ultima catches it in rags that she stores in a bag. Afterward, Antonio is able to keep down some atole, a gruel made of corn meal. Lucas screams in pain, vomiting a squirming mass of hair. When Lucas successfully eats a bowl of atole, Ultima declares the cure finished. The house fills with happy people, but some whisper the words bruja and hechicera (meaning "witch" or "sorceress"). Ultima burns the mass of hair and dirty linen in the grove where Lucas challenged Tenorio's daughters.

SUMMARY: ONCE (11)

Cico offers to take Antonio to see the golden carp. After confirming that Antonio has never fished for a carp, Cico asks Antonio if he believes the golden carp is a god. Crestfallen, Antonio replies that he cannot believe in any god except the god of his church because he is a Catholic. At Cico's request, Antonio swears by the cross that he will never hunt or kill a carp. Afterward, Cico and Antonio visit Narciso's garden, where they eat carrots. Cico explains that Narciso's magic and an underground spring make the garden so lush. Narciso plants by the light of the moon.

Antonio's group of friends invites Antonio and Cico to play ball. Ernie claims that there is a witch living in Antonio's house. Horse asks Antonio to do a magic trick for them. Angry at Ernie's taunting, Antonio agrees. He vomits the carrot juice on the ground, frightening his friends. Cico and Antonio run to a hidden pond where the huge, beautiful golden carp makes its appearance. Cico explains that the carp lives in the Hidden Lakes, a place with a strange power like the presence of the river, but stronger and hungrier. A mermaid lives there, trying to lure men to their deaths. Cico warns Antonio never to go there alone.

Cico explains that the golden carp prophesied that the weight of people's sin would cause the land to sink and be swallowed by the underground lake beneath it. When Antonio replies that it is not fair to the men who don't sin, Cico tells him that all men sin. The story saddens Antonio, and he feels burdened by the knowledge. When he returns home, he learns that Ultima already knows about the golden carp. She tells Antonio that he must find his own truths in adulthood. That night Antonio dreams about the conflicting beliefs he has encountered, as well as the conflict between his parents' wishes for him. Ultima tells Antonio and his parents that the water of the moon and the sea are the same water and that each family member is part of the same cycle.

ANALYSIS: DIEZ–ONCE (10–11)

Antonio's friendship with Samuel initiates Antonio's awareness of the conflicts in his own religion. The El Puerto priest's inability to cure Lucas increases Antonio's doubts. When Ultima successfully cures Lucas, Antonio comes to realize that Ultima's spirituality is both valid and separate from the Catholic Church. Antonio's realization that the church does not have the same kind of power as Ultima suggests to him that no single way of interpreting the world can ever comprehend everything; life requires a commingling of different perspectives, explanations, and beliefs.

In various ways, Anaya symbolically links Antonio's character to the power of healing, showing that Antonio himself may possess some of the spirituality that he admires in Ultima. Mexican folklore traditionally associates Antonio's middle name, Juan, with mystical powers. People who are named Juan are said to have special powers to resist witchcraft. Anaya offers us a vivid description of Ultima's cure, but he does not explain her power. Her power is mysterious—recognizing and honoring its existence is a matter of faith and spirituality.

Part of Ultima's authority in the community and in Antonio's family comes from the fact that even though she is not a member of the Catholic Church, she rigorously follows a philosophy that highly values harmony and free will. She continually contrives to show Antonio how his radically different heritages can coexist harmoniously within him. When she asks Antonio to take part in the cure, for instance, she does so because she knows that he will incur a social cost for helping her, and she wants him to understand what is at stake. This respectful treatment indicates that Ultima believes that Antonio is ready to make independent decisions and accept consequences, the hallmark of adulthood.

Antonio's friends represent the collective social voice, as many people in the community feel that Ultima's cure is witchcraft. Although Antonio maintains his individuality, he still has to deal with social prejudice. Ernie's mean-spirited teasing is Antonio's first real taste of this phenomenon and represents simply another obstacle on his path to wisdom and adulthood. Whereas Ultima is able to understand the multiplicity of life and the incompleteness of any one way of explaining it, Anaya shows that many people are prejudiced by their own views and react to other views with suspicion and fear.

The inability to look past biased assumptions is especially visible in the townspeople's treatment of Narciso. Most people simply view him as the town drunk, and only a few, like Cico, possess the perspective necessary to see that he is actually one of the magic people, like Ultima. Cico's view that Narciso's lush garden is drunk like

Narciso illustrates his idea of tolerance and acceptance, ideals he generally shares with Ultima. Cico's moral order does not condemn Narciso's love of alcohol; instead, he has the ability to see beyond the blinders of social prejudice to see the good in Narciso's magic, just as Antonio does with Ultima. His willingness to be open-minded brings him strength, but also a lot of conflict.

Cico's decision to share the golden carp's apocalyptic prophecy with Antonio illustrates the connection between Cico's religion and Catholicism: both are concerned with moral decadence. The prophecy depresses Antonio because he feels that it burdens him with responsibility, implying that all men sin. As Antonio's dreams about his older brothers reveal, he shoulders a great deal of responsibility for the moral well-being of people close to him. However, Ultima reminds him that he should concentrate on his own fate. She acknowledges the conflict he experiences between the pagan religion and the Catholic Church, but she does not tell him what to believe or what to think. Unlike Antonio's mother, she regards knowledge as the best and most important asset in decision-making.

Antonio's dream about the water of the moon and the water of the sea is a way for him to deal symbolically with the religious conflict between his parents. Gabriel's spiritual beliefs are more like Cico's pagan religion than like María's Catholicism, and the result is even more tension between the parents. Antonio's struggle to cope with competing moral orders is now a symbolic part of his struggle to cope with conflicting family traditions. Ultima, whose character demonstrates the possibility of the harmonious coexistence of opposites, calms Antonio's fears in the dream by revealing the interdependent relationship of the sea and the moon, symbolic representations of his paternal and maternal traditions.

DOCE–TRECE (12–13)

SUMMARY: DOCE (12)

Antonio notices three wax-covered clay dolls on Ultima's shelf. One seems to be bent over in pain. Ultima forbids him to touch the dolls and warns him to stay away from Tenorio. She gives him an amulet containing dried herbs to protect him from danger. One evening, Narciso bursts into the Márez home to report that one of Tenorio's daughters has died. Tenorio told everyone that he found Ultima's little pouch of herbs under his daughter's bed. Narciso warns Ultima that Tenorio is coming with a drunken lynch mob hungry for a witch's death. At that moment, Tenorio and his cohorts arrive. With Antonio at his side, Gabriel demands that they identify themselves and state their business.

To guard against witches, one man has thrust through his lips needles that have been blessed by a priest. Narciso declares that they can pin the needles over Gabriel's door in the sign of a cross. If Ultima is a witch, she cannot walk through the door. The mob agrees to abide by the test. Ultima's owl suddenly gouges out one of Tenorio's eyes. When everyone looks up, Ultima has passed through the door. The mob disperses, but Tenorio vows to kill Ultima. Antonio notices that the needles are no longer pinned above the door. He never finds out if they simply fell or if someone had broken the cross.

SUMMARY: TRECE (13)
Gabriel accompanies his family to El Puerto and stays to take part in the Lunas' harvest for the first time. Antonio ponders the conflicting belief systems of the Catholic Church and the golden carp. He wishes there were a god that always forgave and never punished. He wonders if God is too much like a man. Antonio asks Pedro why he and Antonio's other uncles did not come to warn Ultima like Narciso did. Pedro admits that he was a coward, but he vows to stand by Ultima from now on. Antonio's uncle, Mateo, reports that the surviving Trementina sisters have woven a cottonwood coffin for their dead sister because a witch cannot be buried in a pine, cedar, or piñon coffin. He describes the frightful ceremony for a Black Mass funeral. Antonio has a dream in which Mateo's description of the ceremony is enacted, but when he looks inside the coffin, he finds Ultima. He awakes just in time to see the El Puerto priest refuse to give the dead woman the funeral mass and, therefore, burial in hallowed ground. The whole town witnesses their public shame. Tenorio will never again be able to sway the townspeople to join his vendetta for revenge.

ANALYSIS: DOCE–TRECE (12–13)
Bless Me, Ultima largely describes the process of leaving childhood behind as adult knowledge is acquired. During the remainder of the summer, the anxiety-prone Antonio learns that coping with change and disappointment is a normal part of living, and one that he must accept. At no point does life stop changing. Moreover, change inevitably brings loss and grief, which Antonio learns from watching Gabriel grieve by drinking and muttering to himself angrily because

his sons have rebelled. But change can also bring redemption and forgiveness, which Anaya shows when Gabriel finally begins to understand that his sons must build independent lives and that the Márez spirit he admired in them led them to abandon his dream for their own. By witnessing the drama between Gabriel and his brothers, Antonio learns that rebellion against parental authority is a normal part of becoming an adult.

When Gabriel's old friends from the llano come to town for supplies, Anaya uses their stories as a vehicle for examining the social and economic changes affecting their lifestyles. They demonstrate how railroads and barbed wire are causing the vaquero lifestyle to change and slowly disappear. Antonio listens to the tales of hardship and realizes that his father pines for a life that is already fading. Again, change is shown to be inevitable, and it brings hardship and grief. However, Antonio recognizes that as the vaqueros drink and reminisce about the good old days, they discuss a past that is heavily idealized. María also idealizes her ancestral past—she neglects to mention that the priest who led the Lunas to El Puerto was actually their father. She also idealizes the role of the priest, an important realization for Antonio. He must learn to evaluate truths on his own because other peoples' truths are colored by their personal experiences and losses.

Although Antonio is coming to accept the imperfections in his mother and father, he still has a lot to learn from his parents. Although Gabriel has come to terms with the loss of his old way of life, he retains the vaquero's fierce spirit of independence, as we see when the mob comes for Ultima and he does not hesitate to defend her. Antonio stands by his father's side and learns a valuable lesson in personal integrity. Antonio also learns that not everyone has the courage to stand by his or her convictions when they become unpopular. His Luna uncles did not warn Ultima about Tenorio's evil plans, because they were afraid. Again, Antonio is learning that there are many moral pitfalls in adulthood.

CATORCE (14)

SUMMARY
Antonio returns to school in the fall. Samuel is pleased that Antonio saw the golden carp. He warns Antonio that their classmates will not understand his family's defense of Ultima. When Antonio arrives at the schoolyard, Ernie tries to pick a fight by saying Anto-

nio has a witch in his house. He also shouts that Andrew visits Rosie's house regularly. Antonio ignores the charge against Andrew, but he stands up for Ultima. He and Ernie get into a fight, and before long, everybody is fighting in a pile. The teachers separate the boys, but no one is punished. No one teases Antonio about Ultima afterward.

On the day that Antonio's class is scheduled to give a Christmas play at school, a fierce blizzard covers the ground with snow. Antonio and his rambunctious friends are the only students in their class who show up to school. Their teacher, Miss Violet, decides to have them perform the play in front of the rest of the school anyway. The boys practice all morning, but some of them are not happy at playing the girls' parts. The play becomes a hilarious farce.

Walking home morosely, Antonio sees Tenorio, the saloon-keeper, and Narciso, the town drunk, fighting in the street. Another of Tenorio's daughters is sick. Before stumbling away, Tenorio vows to kill Ultima. Narciso rushes off to find Andrew, one of Antonio's older brothers. Antonio follows Narciso to Rosie's house. To Antonio's horror, Narciso knocks on the door and asks for Andrew. Antonio wonders if the fact that Narciso is looking for Andrew at the brothel means that Andrew has already lost his innocence. When Andrew refuses to take Narciso seriously and warn his parents of Tenorio's threat, Narciso trudges into the blizzard to do it himself. Antonio stays out of sight and follows him.

Antonio hears a pistol shot ring out. He finds Tenorio and Narciso fighting under a juniper tree. When Antonio screams, Tenorio aims at him, but his pistol refuses to fire. After Tenorio flees, Antonio hears Narciso's last confession. He stumbles home to report what he has seen. Antonio falls into a deep fever and dreams that he begs God and the Virgin to forgive Andrew and Narciso. The Virgin replies that she will not forgive Narciso if Antonio does not ask her to forgive Tenorio as well. Antonio cries out for Tenorio to be punished, but God declares that he cannot be a god who is all-giving while taking vengeance on Tenorio at the same time. Antonio cries for God to forgive his own sins.

In his dream, Antonio sees the blood of Lupito and Narciso mix in the river. A mob gathers, calling for Ultima's blood. Antonio's brothers beg him to bless and forgive them. However, they turn into the Trementina sisters when Antonio approaches them. They cut Antonio's hair and mix it with a toad's entrails and a bat's blood. Afterward, they drink it, and Antonio dies despite his mother's prayers and Ultima's magic. Antonio is sentenced to purgatory because he died without taking the Eucharist. Lead by the sisters, a mob kills Ultima, Antonio's family, and Antonio's friends. Afterward, the mob catches and eats carp. A great hole opens in the ground, and water rises out of it, but the sinners take no heed. The sun turns red, and the sinners' skin falls off. When there is no one left alive in Guadalupe, the farmers from El Puerto come to gather the ashes of Antonio and his family. They bury the remains in the holy ground of their fields. The skies clear, and the golden carp swallows everything, good and evil. He ascends to the heavens to become a new sun, shining over a new world.

ANALYSIS

Anaya describes the process of leaving childhood behind not only as the development of a personal belief system, but also the willingness to defend those beliefs. Like his defense of Ultima against the mob in Chapter 12, Antonio's fight with Ernie in Chapter 14 demonstrates his willingness to defend his beliefs even when they are unpopular. Although Gabriel and Ultima clearly influence Antonio's behavior, Antonio's own personal experiences have led him to defend his beliefs as well. Ultima's continual emphasis on the importance of considering different moral frameworks in making decisions certainly affects Antonio, but ultimately, it is Antonio himself who decides what decisions he will make. Understanding that morality cannot be considered absolute or clearly defined gives Antonio greater power to find his own truths. Gabriel's example of fierce individualism gives Antonio the courage to defend the truths he chooses for himself. The golden carp story supports Ultima's lesson that there are multiple but equally valid modes of moral reasoning. In Cico's religion, Narciso is not a moral outcast because of his drinking, for example. Simply knowing this fact gives Antonio the courage to be different.

The episode of the Christmas play shows the multiple ways in which children relate with one another; Antonio's friends are neither entirely negative nor entirely positive forces. Although their teasing can frequently be brutal, they are also able to include Antonio in their games. In contrast to the adult world of the novel, forgiveness is easy to come by among the children. Antonio frequently wrestles with difficult issues in his family life, and his friendships with his classmates function as a way for him to escape those pressures.

Antonio's sighting of Andrew at Rosie's house connects reality with Antonio's earlier unreal dream scene. Although the dream presented an idealized version of Andrew, Antonio is forced to relinquish this image of Andrew when he sees him at Rosie's house. In Antonio's dream, Andrew promises not to enter the brothel until Antonio loses his innocence. If Andrew's entrance into the brothel in this chapter means that Antonio has indeed lost his innocence, then it means that Antonio has lost his childish, innocent worldview, rather than his sexual innocence. As Antonio grows up, he begins to see the complexity of making moral decisions; he is no longer innocently able to assume that right and wrong are absolute categories.

Performing the Catholic Act of Final Contrition for Narciso symbolically places Antonio in the role of priest, connecting Narciso's death to Lupito's, during which Antonio heard Lupito's final confession. With Narciso the experience is different because Antonio personally knows Narciso; Lupito is a stranger. Antonio's dream illustrates how this experience furthers the development of his sense of spirituality and morality. Again, the dream deals with forgiveness, sin, and punishment. The elements of betrayal and vengeance further complicate the matter. It is possible that Andrew's refusal to help Narciso indirectly leads to Narciso's death. The refusal might have led to Antonio's death if Tenorio's gun hadn't misfired. Therefore, Antonio himself is dealing with feelings of betrayal. God's response to Antonio's request that he forgive Andrew is wrathful. Throughout this conflict, God functions in Antonio's dream as an alter ego for Antonio. He symbolizes the part of Antonio that has difficulty forgiving Andrew for letting him down.

Another effect of Antonio's entrance into adolescence is his ability to confront his own imperfections and become curious about religion. Antonio realizes that his desire for vengeance against Tenorio might be unfair. Antonio cannot realistically expect to avoid the darker side of human emotions. Because he dreams that a mob calls out for Ultima's blood, Antonio subconsciously acknowledges that his desire for revenge against Tenorio is just as savage. His dream is also the first in which he himself dies. Antonio's dream also demonstrates that he has gained a greater understanding of Cico's religion. The golden carp's apocalyptic prophecy depressed and frightened him because it seemed so fatalistic. However, his dream shows him how Cico's religion contains the promise of salvation as well.

QUINCE–DIECIOCHO (15–18)

SUMMARY: QUINCE (15)

Antonio is delirious with pneumonia for several days. Narciso's death is declared an accident by the coroner. When Andrew enters Antonio's sickroom, he seems uncomfortable. After he leaves, Ultima assures Antonio that he didn't reveal Andrew's secret in his delirium.

María likes to hear Antonio read prayers in both English and Spanish. Unlike many of their people, she wants her children to know both languages. León and Eugene come to visit for Christmas. They bought a car in Las Vegas but have totaled it during the drive to Guadalupe. The tension between Gabriel and his sons grows. When León and Eugene leave for Sante Fe, Andrew goes with them.

SUMMARY: DIECISÉIS (16)

Antonio hopes that his first Communion will bring him an understanding of why Tenorio's evil goes unpunished. Tenorio confronts Antonio on his way home from school one day. He shouts that another of his daughters is dying and vows to kill Ultima, but he hurries away without harming Antonio. When Antonio reports Tenorio's threats, Ultima assures him that Tenorio won't ambush her as easily as he did Narciso.

SUMMARY: DIECISIETE (17)

Antonio and his friends begin taking catechism lessons with Father Byrnes. That spring, fierce dust storms incite rumors of the atomic bomb. Antonio eagerly looks forward to receiving the knowledge of God. Gabriel laughs when Antonio reports that some people think the atomic bomb has caused the fierce dust storms. He replies that the wind is the voice of the llano. By blowing dust in their faces, it is telling the people that they have sucked the land dry with overgrazing.

Although he doesn't believe in God, Florence attends the catechism lessons because he wants to be with his friends. Florence's mother died when he was three, and his father slowly killed himself with drink. Now his sisters are prostitutes at Rosie's house. He asks Antonio why God would do such things to him. Antonio cannot answer because these are the very questions that haunt Antonio himself. When Antonio and Florence are late to catechism lessons, Father Byrnes punishes Florence but not Antonio. Florence stands patiently in the aisle, holding his arms out to his side, while Bones quietly vandalizes a pew near the oblivious Father Byrnes. Father Byrnes tells a frightening story to explain how long eternity is. He tells the children to imagine that they must move a huge pile of sand across the ocean by allowing a little bird to move one grain of sand at a time. When the bird has finished moving the pile of sand, the first day of eternity has passed.

SUMMARY: DIECIOCHO (18)

Antonio begs Florence to go through with confession and Communion to save himself an eternity in hell. Samuel suggests that the golden carp might be a better god for Florence. They decide to take Florence to see him during the summer.

María buys Antonio a new suit for his first confession and Communion. Antonio's friends decide to make him pretend to be a priest so he can hear their confessions. The children gather around, eager to listen. Horse confesses that he made a hole to see into the girls' bathroom at school. Antonio assigns a penance and remembers the golden carp's prophecy. Bones confesses an even more titillating sin, witnessing two high school students having sex, and Antonio gives him the same penance as Horse. When the children try to force Florence to play along, Florence states that he has no sins because God has sinned against him. The children shrink in horror and suggest beating, stoning, or killing him for his blasphemy. Antonio shouts that he absolves Florence of all his sins. The children fall on Antonio in anger and begin to beat him. They stop only when the priest calls them into the church for confession. Florence tells Antonio that he should have given him a penance, adding that Antonio could never be their priest.

ANALYSIS: QUINCE–DIECIOCHO (15–18)

In these chapters, it becomes clear to Antonio that social prejudice and entrenched assumptions often unfairly determine the course of justice. Because the Catholic mainstream in the town considers Narciso to be nothing more than the town drunk, no one is interested in punishing his murderer. The coroner illustrates this unexamined prejudice when he decides to rule Narciso's death an accident, in defiance of every piece of available evidence. This event teaches Antonio about the tragic unfairness of social prejudice. Antonio also begins to deal with the linguistic component of his cultural identity when María insists that he learn his prayers in English as well as in Spanish. She still hopes that Antonio will be a priest, a spiritual leader for his people, and by insisting that fluency in English and Spanish will make him a better priest, María demonstrates her awareness of the fact that Anglo culture is placing increasing pressures on her own culture. She considers bilingualism a good way to adapt to these changes. Antonio has already felt the sting of Anglo arrogance toward his cultural and ethnic identity at his school.

The conflict between Antonio's maternal and paternal heritages ceases to be his major preoccupation in these chapters, as the main conflict of the novel becomes Antonio's struggle to find a coherent way to understand his experiences. Neither Catholicism nor Ultima's brand of spirituality can completely reflect Antonio's evolving sense of identity and destiny. After society refuses to punish Tenorio for murdering Narciso, Antonio struggles to understand why there is evil in the world. He regards the Catholic Church with both extreme hope and extreme doubt. As a bulwark against these doubts, he places all his hopes on his first Communion, certain that it will bring him complete understanding.

Father Byrnes's unjust punishment of Florence and not Antonio when both boys are late demonstrates to Antonio that even priests can be prejudiced and unfair, and the action undermines Antonio's faith in the goodness of the Catholic Church. However, in Antonio's society the only suggestion that there is room for questioning religious tenets comes from Florence's willingness to question Catholic orthodoxy during classes. Florence's concern is that Father Byrnes's teaching does not give the children a hopeful understanding of God but a fear of him. And despite Father Byrnes's teachings, it is hope that sustains Antonio in the face of doubt and the incontrovertible recognition that there is evil in the world. Antonio desperately wants Florence to have some form of hope as well, a wish he acts on when he agrees with Samuel that perhaps the golden carp will give him hope where the Catholic God has failed.

The authority of the Catholic Church, however, is implicitly undermined by the attitude with which Antonio's friends treat the confession ceremony. The children sensationalize the confessional ritual with sexual voyeurism and compete with one another to confess the worst sin. None of them would probably explicitly acknowledge the element of voyeurism that is inherent in confession, even to themselves. However, their behavior suggests that they have subconsciously recognized that the ceremony has a titillating element. This experience shows Antonio that he may not be suited to life as a priest. Florence does not suggest that it is any failing in Antonio, but rather that his mock congregation is not ready for the kind of priest that Antonio would be.

DIECINUEVE–VENTIUNO (19–21)

SUMMARY: DIECINUEVE (19)

A thousand questions pushed through my mind, but the Voice within me did not answer. There was only silence.
(See QUOTATIONS, *p. 56*)

On Easter Sunday, Antonio takes his first Communion and waits for God to answer the questions that haunt him. However, only silence rings inside his head.

SUMMARY: VEINTE (20)

Antonio continues to attend confession and Communion, but the answers still do not come. The boys from town begin to have gang fights with the boys from Los Jaros. Antonio, who lives between the town and Los Jaros, is caught in the middle. On the last day of school, Antonio calls to Vitamin Kid to race him across the bridge. However, the Vitamin Kid is walking with a girl named Ida, and he expresses no interest in racing.

There is a rumor that Tenorio's sick daughter is near death. Téllez, a rancher from Agua Negra, comes to Ultima to ask help in lifting a curse on his home. Pots and pans fly across the room in his home. Stones rain from the sky. A priest has blessed their house, but the blessing has not been effective. Antonio wonders how an almighty God has again failed to dispel evil. Ultima states that many years ago, Téllez's grandfather hanged three Comanches for raiding his flocks. The curse has awakened the ghosts to force them to do wrong. Gabriel accepts responsibility for interfering with destiny if Ultima helps his friends.

Gabriel and Antonio accompany Ultima to Agua Negra. Antonio realizes that María teaches him that every man is tied to the earth in his need for nourishment and security, but Ultima and Gabriel teach him that the land serves a more spiritual function: immortality comes from freedom, and freedom is nourished by the land, air, and sea.

When they arrive, Ultima instructs Antonio and Gabriel to build a platform in the yard and to cover it with juniper branches. Ultima asks Gabriel to place three bundles on the platform and set it all on fire. Gabriel informs Antonio that his father once told him that the Comanche burned their dead on platforms like this. When the platform is burned completely, Ultima declares that the curse is lifted. Téllez mentions that a month earlier he challenged Tenorio for speaking badly of Ultima. Soon thereafter, the evil things began to occur in his home.

That night, Antonio dreams that his brothers call for him to give them rest from their restless sea-blood. Antonio replies that he cannot help them. He baits his hook with their livers and begins to fish in the river. They continue to cry out, so he unbaits his hook and throws their livers into the River of the Carp. Finally, they rest.

SUMMARY: VEINTIUNO (21)
Antonio and Cico decide the time is right to take Florence to see the golden carp. Antonio confesses his doubts about the God of the Catholic Church. Cico explains that there are many gods, and that Antonio's god is jealous. Antonio will have to choose between the carp and the God of the Church. They find their friends waving excitedly at them next to the shores of the Blue Lake in the section where swimming is forbidden. Horse shouts that Florence hasn't emerged from the water. Just as Cico prepares to dive for Florence, Florence's body floats to the surface. Antonio prays the Act of Contrition over Florence's body but despairs that it is useless because Florence never believed. When the lifeguards finally arrive, Horse and the others lie and say they tried to persuade Florence not to swim in the forbidden area. Sickened, Antonio runs along the river.

ANALYSIS: DIECINUEVE–VENTIUNO (19–21)
Antonio's intensified religious doubts illustrate the extent to which he had pegged his hope for moral understanding on a miraculous epiphany during his Communion. His disillusionment indicates the degree to which Antonio is still a child, even if he is an unusually thoughtful and morally curious one. It is naïve, of course, for him to think that the act of receiving Communion might revolutionize his moral understanding of the world, but his power of understanding and belief is still so strong that he is able to convince himself completely. However, his childlike faith takes a blow after his disappointment. After repeated failures to receive God's explanation of the existence of evil, Antonio even ventures the thought that God himself does not exist. His faith in God is further challenged when

Ultima is able to lift the curse on Téllez's home, an act a priest failed spectacularly to accomplish.

The novel describes the process of entering adolescence as involving a loss that is to be mourned, but to which children must resign themselves. Antonio senses that his friends are also undergoing a lot of change, and this section begins to dramatize the turmoil of adolescence, symbolizing the fact that Antonio really is growing up. Like all the book's depicted life changes, adolescence brings a share of loss and regret, as we see when the Vitamin Kid does not want to race anymore and when Antonio mourns the loss of "something good." Nevertheless, he accepts the changes in his friends and his relationship with them as inevitable, indicating his broad perspective and his courageous determination to adapt to the changes he faces.

Antonio's despair of understanding why evil exists actually leads him to greater spiritual understanding. As a result of his failed religious inquiry, Antonio finds a sort of peace in his spiritual relationship with the land and nature. He owes his multifaceted appreciation of these things to the different influences of his mother, his father, and Ultima. Antonio has finally achieved a kind of harmony regarding his radically different heritages. His ability to enjoy peacefully the land's beauty provides him with respite from the unanswerable question of evil. He also finds respite in the multiplicity of religious traditions: at the moment his confidence in Catholicism wanes to almost nothing, Antonio begins going again with Cico to wait for the golden carp. While watching the golden carp, Antonio achieves a sense of peace that Catholicism does not give him. The golden carp allows him to appreciate the beauty of the moment, soothing his constant anxiety regarding the existence of evil; the power of the carp to soothe him indicates that, as Ultima believes, the idea of a religious tradition is not an all-or-nothing principle. It is possible to appreciate the truths that lie within a tradition of Catholicism without being utterly devastated when they prove incomplete, because there are other traditions in the world, and each can answer questions that the others leave blank.

Antonio assumes the role of a priest for the third time, and this time signals his final loss of hope in the Catholic church. Tragically, Florence dies just before Antonio and Cico can initiate him into the religion of the golden carp. In this scene, Antonio performs as a priest by reciting the Act of Final Contrition for Florence, but he has no sense of hope while he does so. In addition to the tragedy of seeing a friend die, Antonio is also exposed to the nastier side of human moral weakness when the lifeguard on duty yells at the boys for ruining his "perfect record."

VEINTIDÓS (22)

SUMMARY

The tragic consequences of life can be overcome by the magical strength that resides in the human heart.

(See QUOTATIONS, *p. 57*)

As Antonio sleeps, Lupito, Narciso, and Florence appear in Antonio's dreams. They say that Antonio prayed the Act of Final Contrition for them "in his innocence" even though they were outcasts. When Antonio asks why he must see so much violence, a voice tells him that creation lies in violence. Antonio watches a priest defile an altar with pigeon's blood and Cico defile the river with the golden carp's blood. He has a vision of Tenorio murdering Ultima by killing her "night-spirit." Antonio cries out, "My God, my God, why have you forsaken me!" Narciso, Florence, and Lupito tell Antonio that they live only in his dreams. When Antonio awakes, Ultima suggests that he go to his uncles in El Puerto. Antonio has seen too much death. His uncles can teach him about growing life. Before he leaves, Ultima advises him to be ready to make life's changes part of his strength.

Gabriel explains that he does not mind sending Antonio to María's brothers because he will still be with men who can guide him into manhood. He admits that the vaquero's way of life is fading, so he is ready to end the long conflict with María. Antonio replies that he wants to be both a Luna and a Márez. Gabriel explains that every man takes his past and makes something new with it. As Antonio muses out loud that it is possible to make a new religion, he asks his father if the priest who led the Lunas to El Puerto was actually their father in more than the metaphorical sense. Gabriel confirms his suspicions.

When Antonio asks why there is evil in the world, Gabriel replies that people call things they do not understand "evil." He explains that understanding comes only with life experience. He says that acquiring knowledge is not as easy as swallowing the host at Communion. He believes that Ultima's magic comes from the understanding she has gained from her years of working with the sick and the frightened.

During the summer with his Luna uncles, Antonio's nightmares cease to disturb his sleep. Although Antonio does not know what his future holds, he is glad to learn the Luna way of life. When Tenorio's sick daughter dies at the end of the summer, he vows to everyone who will listen that he will kill Ultima. Pedro resolves to stand by Ultima this time. He tells Antonio that they must drive to Guadalupe directly after supper, so he sends Antonio to Prudencio's house to pack for the journey home.

During the walk to Prudencio's home, Tenorio tries to trample Antonio with his horse. Antonio throws himself down the embankment to hide in the bushes by the river. Tenorio shouts that the owl is Ultima's spirit, so he plans to kill Ultima by killing the owl. Antonio runs ten miles to Guadalupe to warn Ultima. When he reaches his parents' house, Pedro's car screeches to a halt in front of the house. Gabriel runs to the door and asks what has happened. Pedro asks if they have seen Antonio.

Meanwhile, Antonio spies Tenorio near a juniper tree. When Antonio shouts a warning, Tenorio aims a rifle at him. Ultima calls her owl, and it attacks Tenorio. Tenorio shoots it during the struggle and aims his gun at Antonio again. Before he can kill Antonio, Pedro shoots Tenorio dead. Antonio takes the dying owl to Ultima's bedside. Ultima explains that her teacher told her to do good works but not to interfere with destiny. Her death and Tenorio's death are simply the restoration of the original harmony. She tells Antonio that he must burn all of her possessions at sunrise. Tonight, he must bury the owl next to a forked juniper tree. Before she dies, Ultima blesses Antonio "in the name of all that is good and strong and beautiful." He goes and buries the owl.

*Love life, and if despair enters your heart, look for me in
the evenings when the wind is gentle and the owls sing in
the hills. I shall be with you—"*

(See QUOTATIONS, *p. 58*)

*In two days we would celebrate the mass of the dead,
and after mass we would take her body to the cemetery
in Las Pasturas for burial. But all that would only be the
ceremony that was prescribed by custom. Ultima was
really buried here. Tonight.*

(See QUOTATIONS, *p. 59*)

ANALYSIS

Antonio's final dream addresses his crisis of religious faith. The
three people he tries to save present declarations in his dream that
each follow the same pattern: first, they state that Antonio prayed
for them in his innocence; then they proceed to show him the failure
of all three spiritual paradigms in his life. The dream hints at Antonio's understanding that people often disobey the rules of their own
religions. His dream also foreshadows the manner of Ultima's
death. Seeing the failure of all three spiritual paradigms, Antonio
asks God why he has forsaken him, a question that echoes Jesus'
last words on the cross and illustrates the depth of Antonio's
anguished doubt.

The voice that breaks into Antonio's dream, reminding Antonio
that violence is the seed of creation, suggests that Antonio must
learn to accept that violence brings change, and, in fact, that change
is a kind of violence. This viewpoint supports the novel's argument
that the transition into adulthood requires a person to develop the
kind of faith that can accept doubt, contradiction, and loss in the
absence of absolute answers. Ultima continues to act as Antonio's
mentor as she advises his parents to send him to his uncles to learn
about "growing life." She also reiterates the novel's concern with
violence as a part of change when, before Antonio leaves, she
advises him that he must learn to accept change and make it a
part of his strength.

Antonio's conversation with his father signals Antonio's depar-
ture from absolute modes of thinking. Gabriel has finally come to
terms with the sweeping changes that are destroying the vaquero
way of life. Antonio learns that adults face change their whole lives,
and Gabriel's assertion that every man builds something new from

his past echoes Ultima's statement that Antonio has to make change a part of his strength.

Antonio's final separation from Ultima is also a test of the lessons that she has taught him regarding the ambiguity of good and evil. When the battle between Ultima and Tenorio comes to its violent end, Antonio has reason to remember his father's relativist attitude toward evil. Antonio finally begins to understand the spiritual value that Ultima places on harmony. After he affirms both his Luna and Márez heritages, he feels at peace with his identity, and his sense of peace helps him to understand what Anaya has intended to show us all along, that his maternal and paternal heritages are compatible. He ceases to see them in terms of incompatible opposites but as opposites in a balanced unity. This is how he comes to understand the cycle of life and death as well so that death ceases to be an evil thing. Antonio regards it as another change that brings grief. This time, he recognizes that change can also bring wisdom and a deeper understanding.

IMPORTANT QUOTATIONS EXPLAINED

1.   The orange of the golden carp appeared at the edge of the
     pond. . . . We watched in silence at the beauty and grandeur
     of the great fish. Out of the corners of my eyes I saw Cico
     hold his hand to his breast as the golden carp glided by. Then
     with a switch of his powerful tail the golden carp
     disappeared into the shadowy water under the thicket.

This quotation from Chapter 11 is Antonio's description of his first
sighting of the golden carp. The quotation is important because it
represents Antonio's most significant confrontation with a non-
Christian faith. Stylistically, it is also an important example of how
Anaya adapts his prose style to the emotional and psychological
contexts of his characters' situations. The golden carp is a natural,
pagan deity compared to the Christian God Antonio is used to wor-
shipping.

   Anaya depicts the carp in a poetic style that emphasizes its awe-
inspiring beauty, rather than focus immediately on the crisis of faith
that the carp causes for Antonio. The language Anaya uses to
describe the carp is simple, elemental, and powerful. Anaya chooses
to have the narrator describe the carp rather than have Antonio tell
us about it. This distance conveys the reverence that the carp
inspires in the boys, who observe the carp in transfixed silence. Cico
even puts his hand on his heart, a subtle gesture that conveys the
depth of feeling that the carp inspires in the boys.

2.   God! Why did Lupito die? Why do you allow the evil of the
      Trementinas? Why did you allow Narciso to be murdered
      when he was doing good? . . . A thousand questions pushed
      through my mind, but the Voice within me did not answer. .
      . . The mass was ending, the fleeting mystery was already
      vanishing.

This quotation from Chapter 19 depicts Antonio's first Communion. The ceremony contrasts sharply with Antonio's experience
with the golden carp in Chapter 11. When Antonio sees the carp, he
witnesses something elemental, magical, and miraculous without
much effort and without immediately understanding its intellectual
consequences. At his first Communion, Antonio attempts to experience a similar epiphany, but he tries so hard and is so full of questions and anxiety that nothing happens, and he is left disappointed.
Antonio's immediate, aggressive questioning of God, which begins
as soon as he swallows the Communion wafer, is indicative of the
impact of his moral quandaries—he is so anxious to discover the
answers to his questions that he attempts to shout God down from
heaven to ask him. His failure to find God is a further indication of
the limitations of Catholicism, or indeed of any single religious system, to provide the answers to all of life's questions. Antonio must
learn to draw his own conclusions and to think for himself. He must
learn to live in a world in which Catholicism and the golden carp can
coexist, and he must grow to impart knowledge and enlightenment
from all the spiritual forces in his life.

3. The tragic consequences of life can be overcome by the magical strength that resides in the human heart.

This sentence sums up the major thematic claim of *Bless Me, Ultima*—through all of life's injustices and hardships, the power of the human heart prevails. Antonio has this realization in Chapter 22, when he realizes what Ultima has been trying to teach him all along. Antonio can experience the suffering of his friends and family and the string of tragic deaths that he witnesses, and still persevere and thrive. This quotation also resolves the tension between innocence and experience that arises from the moment that María first claims that it is a sin to grow up. Innocence is fleeting, but the "magical strength" of the heart is not. This "magical strength," and not innocence, is the ultimate source of human goodness and hope.

4.   I bless you in the name of all that is good and strong and
      beautiful, Antonio. Always have the strength to live. Love
      life, and if despair enters your heart, look for me in the
      evenings when the wind is gentle and the owls sing in the
      hills. I shall be with you—

Ultima's final blessing to Antonio in Chapter 22 clarifies *Bless Me,
Ultima*'s moral standpoint. Ultima's explicit association of her spirit
with nature as she refers to the gentle wind, the singing owls, and the
evenings, indicates her spiritual conviction about the connections
that bind all living things. Her statement also gives Antonio a framework with which to understand her death by offering a sequence of
physical objects that he can see as symbols of her life and through
which he can continue to feel her presence. Antonio will be without
Ultima and will have to make his own choices without her guidance
from now on, but she makes it clear in this blessing that her spirit
will endure with him and that the lessons she has taught him will still
serve him well even after she dies.

5. In two days we would celebrate the mass of the dead, and after mass we would take her body to the cemetery in Las Pasturas for burial. But all that would only be the ceremony that was prescribed by custom. Ultima was really buried here. Tonight.

As Antonio buries Ultima's owl in Chapter 22, he decides that he is really burying Ultima as well. Antonio's statement emphasizes the conflict between the practices of Catholicism and indigenous mysticism. The Catholic burial offers one view of death, and the mystical burial of the owl presents another. Now, instead of feeling that he has to choose between the two, Antonio accepts both views positively. He can look forward to "the ceremony that was prescribed by custom" without feeling as though he is betraying God by believing that the burial of the owl is more spiritually significant than a Catholic ceremony. He can draw from each tradition and, as Ultima has taught him, become a stronger, better person as a result.

KEY FACTS

FULL TITLE
Bless Me, Ultima

AUTHOR
Rudolfo A. Anaya

TYPE OF WORK
Novel

GENRE
Bildungsroman (coming-of-age story); magical realism

LANGUAGE
English, with Spanish words and phrases throughout

TIME AND PLACE WRITTEN
1960s, Albuquerque, New Mexico

DATE OF FIRST PUBLICATION
1972

PUBLISHER
Quinto Sol Publishers

NARRATOR
Antonio as an adult, recounting a few years of his childhood

POINT OF VIEW
The novel is written exclusively from Antonio's first-person
point of view.

TONE
For the most part, the narrator's tone is serious and lyrical, with
simple, poetic language used to depict Antonio's weighty
philosophical struggles. The tone of the novel generally matches
the mood of its main character.

TENSE
Past

SETTINGS (TIME)
Mid-1940s, during and after World War II

SETTINGS (PLACE)
Guadalupe, New Mexico, and its surrounding area

PROTAGONIST
Antonio

MAJOR CONFLICT
As Antonio moves from childhood to adolescence, he tries to reconcile his parents' and his community's conflicting cultural traditions; Antonio's goal is independent thought and action; he strives to make his own moral decisions and to accept responsibility for their consequences.

RISING ACTION
After Ultima arrives to stay with Antonio's family, Antonio witnesses the murder of Lupito, a local man. He also experiences mounting anxiety over going away to school and leaving his mother.

CLIMAX
Ultima cures Lucas's illness, presumably caused by Tenorio's daughters, whom he saw participating in a satanic ritual. By curing Lucas, Ultima incites Tenorio's rage, and Tenorio vows to kill Ultima.

FALLING ACTION
Antonio goes to school and builds friendships there. Tenorio, still angry with Ultima, kills the pet owl that guides her in her magic healing. When the owl dies, Ultima dies as well. She asks Antonio to bury the owl's body.

THEMES
The importance of moral independence; the influence of culture on identity

MOTIFS
Dreams; family; learning and education; tolerance and understanding

SYMBOLS
The golden carp; Ultima's owl; the Virgin of Guadalupe

FORESHADOWING
Antonio's dreams; Ultima's comments about the future

STUDY QUESTIONS & ESSAY TOPICS

STUDY QUESTIONS

1. *How do María's and Gabriel's attitudes regarding the process of growing up relate to Antonio's future?*

María associates growing up with learning how to sin, but Gabriel and Ultima view growing up as an inevitable process that is neither good nor bad. María believes that as a boy becomes a man, he uses his life experience and his knowledge to make decisions. She also believes that Antonio will be saved only if he becomes a priest. María even wants to go to Father Byrnes to discuss Antonio's future as a priest. Gabriel sharply disagrees, arguing that no one but Antonio should decide whether he becomes a priest. Gabriel's response reveals his staunch belief that destiny should be determined by one's own thoughts and actions, not by outsiders or imposing family members. María, a staunch Catholic, believes she must guide Antonio's future carefully because his soul is at stake. She also has a selfish motive: if she releases control over him, Antonio will start to make his own decisions and will no longer look to her for guidance.

2. *Antonio struggles to choose between his maternal and paternal heritages. What are the conflicts within his parents' heritages?*

María's family is devoutly Catholic, and their greatest hope is that Antonio will become a priest. The spiritual character of their relationship to the earth is closely tied to indigenous religion, while their devotion to Catholicism represents the extent to which European culture has shaped them. They plant by the cycles of the moon. Luna, the Spanish word for moon, illustrates symbolically how deeply this spiritual relationship is rooted in the family's identity. Despite the violent clash between Spanish and indigenous religions, María's culture contains harmonious elements of both.

On the other hand, Gabriel's family favors the vaquero, or cowboy, way of life. His family is driven by the same adventurous, restless spirit that drove the Spaniards across the ocean to the New World, as conveyed by their family name, which is derived from the Spanish word for ocean. Gabriel's worldview is heavily influenced by indigenous culture as well. Like the Luna family, he has a strong spiritual and mystical relationship with the land. The Lunas see the opportunity to build towns in the vast expanse of the llano. Gabriel's family views the llano with reverence and deference; they want its wildness preserved because for them it represents their heritage and the struggles and hardship they have endured.

3.   *How does seeing Andrew at Rosie's house affect Antonio's opinion of Andrew?*

Antonio is forced to relinquish his idealized image of Andrew when he sees him at Rosie's house. Originally, when Ernie teases Antonio about Andrew's visits to the brothel, Antonio ignores the comments, refusing to believe that his brother visits a brothel. However, when Antonio later sees Andrew at the brothel, he is forced to accept the truth. This confrontation makes real a dream of Antonio's in which Andrew promises not to enter the brothel until Antonio loses his innocence. If Andrew's entrance into the brothel signifies that the dream has become a reality, then Antonio must have also lost his innocence. However, Antonio's loss of innocence does not necessarily mean he has sinned. It might suggest instead that Antonio is no longer in denial about Andrew's behavior and that he acknowledges the power of physical desire, which Antonio will eventually feel as well.

4.   *Antonio has a dream in which the golden carp's prophecy comes true. How does his dream demonstrate Antonio's growing understanding of the religion of the golden carp?*

The golden carp's apocalyptic prophecy frightens and saddens Antonio at first because it seems so fatalistic. Catholicism offers the chance of salvation through communion with God, but Antonio does not perceive any chance for salvation in Cico's religion. Instead, Antonio sees the entire town destroyed by degenerate sinners, just as the golden carp's prophecy predicts. However, his dream shows him that Cico's religion might also contain a promise of salvation. The golden carp swallows everything, both good and evil. Afterward, the world is reborn. The prospect of rebirth promises moral purification in Cico's religion. Moral purification simply occurs in a different way in Cico's religion than it does in Catholicism.

5. *When Ultima blesses Antonio on his first day of school, he feels the power of a whirlwind surround him. How does local folklore regard whirlwinds? What realization do whirlwinds help Antonio make about good and evil?*

Local folklore refers to whirlwinds as dust devils, an evil phenomenon against the will of God. As a result, the sign of the cross is supposed to ward off dust devils. Ultima's blessing reminds Antonio of the time he let a whirlwind knock him to the ground, and he wonders if the powers of good and evil have the same origin. At this point, Antonio understands that power in itself does not have a moral component. Instead, how people use their powers determines their moral status.

SUGGESTED ESSAY TOPICS

1. Both Ultima and Narciso are called "magic" by various
    characters in the book. Compare and contrast the characters
    of Ultima and Narciso. How does Ultima's brand of magic
    differ from Narciso's? How are they alike? In what sense
    might each character be called "magic"?

2. What does Antonio learn from his conversation with Gabriel
    during the trip to El Puerto after Florence's death? How does
    this lesson help to prepare him for the challenges that lie
    ahead?

3. What is the significance of the conflict between English-
    speakers and Spanish-speakers that Antonio encounters at
    school? Why is language so important in the novel? In what
    sense does this conflict give Antonio perspective on the
    conflict within his family?

4. In María's view, how are sexuality, adulthood, and sin
    related? Why is childhood preferable to adulthood? How do
    these factors influence her desire for Antonio to become a
    priest? And how does María's own childhood influence her
    current beliefs?

5. What does Antonio learn from watching Gabriel cope with
    the rebellion of Antonio's brothers?

Review & Resources

Quiz

1. What is the llano?

    A. The plains of New Mexico
    B. A magical song
    C. The plaintive song of a dove
    D. A legendary mountain

2. What is a vaquero?

    A. A singer who sings the llano
    B. A dancer who dances the llano
    C. A cowboy who rides on the llano
    D. A bird that lives on the llano

3. How old is Antonio at the start of the novel?

    A. Ten
    B. Six
    C. Twelve
    D. Fourteen

4. In which war do Antonio's brothers fight?

    A. Vietnam
    B. The Civil War
    C. The Spanish-American War
    D. World War II

5. What language do Antonio's sisters prefer to speak?

    A. English
    B. Navajo
    C. Spanish
    D. Comanche

6.   Who is with Antonio when he sees the golden carp?

   A.   Narciso
   B.   Gabriel
   C.   Ultima
   D.   Cico

7.   What do Antonio and Ultima do on their long walks together?

   A.   Sing songs
   B.   Gather herbs
   C.   Hunt animals
   D.   Plot Antonio's future

8.   How do most people characterize Narciso?

   A.   As a magical person
   B.   As the local criminal
   C.   As the town's strongest man
   D.   As the town drunk

9.   Where does Antonio first see the golden carp?

   A.   A secluded pond
   B.   María's garden
   C.   The school
   D.   Ultima's garden

10.   What kind of bird does Ultima have as a familiar?

   A.   A crow
   B.   A hawk
   C.   An owl
   D.   A kestrel

11.   How does Tenorio kill Ultima?

   A.   He stabs her
   B.   He shoots her animal familiar
   C.   He shoots her
   D.   He cuts off her head

12. Which character does not believe in God?

    A. Narciso
    B. Antonio
    C. María
    D. Florence

13. Which character drowns?

    A. Florence
    B. María
    C. Antonio
    D. Narciso

14. Who kills Narciso?

    A. Florence
    B. Gabriel
    C. Tenorio
    D. A Japanese soldier

15. Who kills Lupito?

    A. Gabriel
    B. A mob
    C. The sheriff
    D. Narciso

16. Who kills the sheriff?

    A. Gabriel
    B. Narciso
    C. Antonio
    D. Lupito

17. Where does Gabriel hope to move his family?

    A. New York City
    B. California
    C. Mexico City
    D. Far Hills

18. What does God say to Antonio during his first Communion?

    A. "I am within thee."
    B. "The answers are within thee."
    C. Nothing
    D. "Search thyself."

19. What are the Lunas?

    A. Farmers
    B. Bakers
    C. Cowboys
    D. Evening spirits

20. What sins does Florence say he has committed?

    A. Lust and sloth
    B. Lust and greed
    C. Sloth and envy
    D. None

21. Why does Antonio decide that Andrew is not a good model for him?

    A. He drinks too much
    B. He beats his wife in front of Cico
    C. He cannot sing the llano
    D. He refuses to leave the brothel to help Ultima

22. What character is the only person the Indian will talk to?

    A. Cico
    B. Jáson
    C. María
    D. Antonio

23. Where does Antonio sleep in the house?

    A. The basement
    B. A bedroom with Andrew
    C. The attic
    D. The cupboard under the stairs

24. What do Antonio's sisters like to do for fun?

    A.   Play with dolls
    B.   Cook
    C.   Flirt with boys
    D.   Wrestle

25. Who buries the owl?

    A.   Gabriel
    B.   Ultima
    C.   Tenorio
    D.   Antonio

ANSWER KEY:

1: A; 2: C; 3: B; 4: D; 5: A; 6: D; 7: B; 8: D; 9: A; 10: C; 11: B; 12: D;
13: A; 14: C; 15: B; 16: D; 17: B; 18: C; 19: C; 20: D; 21: D; 22: B; 23: B;
24: A; 25: D

SUGGESTIONS FOR FURTHER READING

ANAYA, RUDOLFO A. *Tortuga: A Novel*. Albuquerque: University of New Mexico Press, 1988.

———— AND FRANCISCO LOMELI, EDS. *Aztlan: Essays on the Chicano Homeland*. Albuquerque: University of New Mexico Press, 1991.

DARDER, ANTONIA AND RODOLFO D. TORRES, EDS. *The Latino Studies Reader: Culture, Economy, and Society*. Malden, Massachusetts: Blackwell Publishers, 1998.

DEUTSCH, SARAH. *No Separate Refuge: Culture, Class, and Gender on an Anglo-Hispanic frontier in the American Southwest, 1880–1940*. New York: Oxford University Press, 1987.

FENDER, STEPHEN. *Plotting the Golden West: American Literature and the Rhetoric of the California Trail*. New York: Cambridge University Press, 1981.

GRACIA JORGE J.E. AND PABLO DE GREIFF, EDS. *Hispanics /Latinos in the United States: Ethnicity, Race, and Rights*. New York: Routledge, 2000.

LATTIN, VERNON E., ED. *Contemporary Chicano Fiction: A Critical Survey*. Tempe, Arizona: Bilingual Press, 1986.

SparkNotes
Test Preparation
Guides

The SparkNotes team figured it was time to cut standardized tests down to size. We've studied the tests for you, so that SparkNotes test prep guides are:

Smarter
Packed with critical-thinking skills and test-
taking strategies that will improve your score.

Better
Fully up to date, covering all new features of the tests,
with study tips on every type of question.

Faster
Our books cover exactly what you need to
know for the test. No more, no less.

SparkNotes Guide to the SAT & PSAT
SparkNotes Guide to the SAT & PSAT—Deluxe Internet Edition
SparkNotes Guide to the ACT
SparkNotes Guide to the ACT—Deluxe Internet Edition
SparkNotes SAT Verbal Workbook
SparkNotes SAT Math Workbook
SparkNotes Guide to the SAT II Writing
5 More Practice Tests for the SAT II Writing
SparkNotes Guide to the SAT II U.S. History
5 More Practice Tests for the SAT II History
SparkNotes Guide to the SAT II Math Ic
5 More Practice Tests for the SAT II Math Ic
SparkNotes Guide to the SAT II Math IIc
5 More Practice Tests for the SAT II Math IIc
SparkNotes Guide to the SAT II Biology
5 More Practice Tests for the SAT II Biology
SparkNotes Guide to the SAT II Physics

SparkNotes™ Literature Guides

1984

The Adventures of Huckleberry Finn

The Adventures of Tom Sawyer

The Aeneid

All Quiet on the Western Front

And Then There Were None

Angela's Ashes

Animal Farm

Anna Karenina

Anne of Green Gables

Anthem

Antony and Cleopatra

Aristotle's Ethics

As I Lay Dying

As You Like It

Atlas Shrugged

The Awakening

The Autobiography of Malcolm X

The Bean Trees

The Bell Jar

Beloved

Beowulf

Billy Budd

Black Boy

Bless Me, Ultima

The Bluest Eye

Brave New World

The Brothers Karamazov

The Call of the Wild

Candide

The Canterbury Tales

Catch-22

The Catcher in the Rye

The Chocolate War

The Chosen

Cold Mountain

Cold Sassy Tree

The Color Purple

The Count of Monte Cristo

Crime and Punishment

The Crucible

Cry, the Beloved Country

Cyrano de Bergerac

David Copperfield

Death of a Salesman

The Death of Socrates

The Diary of a Young Girl

A Doll's House

Don Quixote

Dr. Faustus

Dr. Jekyll and Mr. Hyde

Dracula

Dune

East of Eden

Edith Hamilton's Mythology

Emma

Ethan Frome

Fahrenheit 451

Fallen Angels

A Farewell to Arms

Farewell to Manzanar

Flowers for Algernon

For Whom the Bell Tolls

The Fountainhead

Frankenstein

The Giver

The Glass Menagerie

Gone With the Wind

The Good Earth

The Grapes of Wrath

Great Expectations

The Great Gatsby

Greek Classics

Grendel

Gulliver's Travels

Hamlet

The Handmaid's Tale

Hard Times

Harry Potter and the Sorcerer's Stone

Heart of Darkness

Henry IV, Part I

Henry V

Hiroshima

The Hobbit

The House of Seven Gables

I Know Why the Caged Bird Sings

The Iliad

Inferno

Inherit the Wind

Invisible Man

Jane Eyre

Johnny Tremain

The Joy Luck Club

Julius Caesar

The Jungle

The Killer Angels

King Lear

The Last of the Mohicans

Les Miserables

A Lesson Before Dying

The Little Prince

Little Women

Lord of the Flies

The Lord of the Rings

Macbeth

Madame Bovary

A Man for All Seasons

The Mayor of Casterbridge

The Merchant of Venice

A Midsummer Night's Dream

Moby Dick

Much Ado About Nothing

My Antonia

Narrative of the Life of Frederick Douglass

Native Son

The New Testament

Night

Notes from Underground

The Odyssey

The Oedipus Plays

Of Mice and Men

The Old Man and the Sea

The Old Testament

Oliver Twist

The Once and Future King

One Day in the Life of Ivan Denisovich

One Flew Over the Cuckoo's Nest

One Hundred Years of Solitude

Othello

Our Town

The Outsiders

Paradise Lost

A Passage to India

The Pearl

The Picture of Dorian Gray

Poe's Short Stories

A Portrait of the Artist as a Young Man

Pride and Prejudice

The Prince

A Raisin in the Sun

The Red Badge of Courage

The Republic

Richard III

Robinson Crusoe

Romeo and Juliet

The Scarlet Letter

A Separate Peace

Silas Marner

Sir Gawain and the Green Knight

Slaughterhouse-Five

Snow Falling on Cedars

Song of Solomon

The Sound and the Fury

Steppenwolf

The Stranger

Streetcar Named Desire

The Sun Also Rises

A Tale of Two Cities

The Taming of the Shrew

The Tempest

Tess of the d'Ubervilles

Their Eyes Were Watching God

Things Fall Apart

The Things They Carried

To Kill a Mockingbird

To the Lighthouse

Treasure Island

Twelfth Night

Ulysses

Uncle Tom's Cabin

Walden

War and Peace

Wuthering Heights

A Yellow Raft in Blue Water